DR. ASHLEY LITTLE

A Message from the Founder
Dr. Ashley Little

Historically Black Colleges & Universities (HBCUs) were established to serve the educational needs of black Americans. During the time of their establishment, and many years afterward, blacks were generally denied admission to traditionally white institutions. Prior to The Civil War, there was no structured higher education system for black students. Public policy, and certain statutory provisions, prohibited the education of blacks in various parts of the nation. Today, HBCUs represent a vital component of American higher education.

The HBCU Experience Movement, LLC is a collection of stories from prominent alumni throughout the world, who share how their HBCU experience molded them into the people they are today. We are also investing financially into HBCUs throughout the country. Our goal is to create a global movement of prominent HBCU alumni throughout the nation to continue to share their stories each year, allowing us to give back to prestigious HBCUs annually.

We are proud to present to you *The HBCU Experience: The Prairie View A&M University Edition*. We would like to acknowledge and give a special thanks to our amazing lead author, Kayla Robinson, for your dedication and commitment. We appreciate you and thank you for your hard work and dedication on behalf of this project. We would also like to give a special thanks to our foreword author, expert author, contributing authors and partners of Prairie View A&M University for believing in this movement and investing your time, and monetary donations, to give back to your school. We appreciate all of the Prairie View A&M University alumni who shared your HBCU experience in this publication.

About Dr. Ashley Little

Dr. Ashley Little is The CEO/Founder of Ashley Little Enterprises, LLC which encompasses her Media, Consulting Work, Writing, Ghost Writing, Book Publishing, Book Coaching, Project Management, Magazine, Public Relations & Marketing, and Empowerment Speaking. In addition, she is an Award-Winning Serial Entrepreneur, TV/Radio Host, TEDx Speaker, International Speaker, Keynote Speaker, Media Maven, Journalist, Writer, Host, Philanthropist, Business Coach, Investor, Advisor for She Wins Society and 15X Award-Winning Best Selling Author. As seen on Black Enterprise(2X), Forbes (2X), Sheen Magazine (Print and Online), Sheen Talk, Voyage ATL, Fox Soul TV, NBC, Fox, CBS, BlackNews.Com, Shoutout Miami, Shoutout Atlanta, TEDx Speaker, Morning Star, Yahoo Finance, Heart and Soul, The Book of Sean, HBCU Times, VIP Global Magazine, The Black Report, Vocal, Ted.com, Medium, Soul Wealth, Hustle and Soul, BlackBusiness.com, Glambitious Top 21 Women Of 2021, New York Weekly's Top 10 Hardest Working CEOs alongside Billionaire Mark Cuban, US Insiders Top 10 Women Entrepreneurs alongside Billionaire and Media Mogul Oprah Winfrey, London Daily Post, Sheen Magazine 5 Pioneers Making A Difference In Their Communities, NCA&T Alumni Times, CEO Weekly Top 10 Influential People In 2021 alongside Billionaires Jeff Bezos and Beyonce' and many more. Through the Biden & Harris Administration and Leaders Esteem Christian Bible University she was also awarded with the Presidential Lifetime Achievement Award. Also, she is a Board Member for Leaders Esteem Christian Bible University as well.

Next, she is a recipient of the "Author of The Year" award by Glambitious. She is also apart of The Forbes Next 1000 Class of

2021 in partnership with Square. This first-of-its-kind initiative celebrates bold and inspiring entrepreneurs who are redefining what it means to run a business. Furthermore, she is a recipient of Nashville's Black 40 Under 40 Awards December 2021 it is an annual event honoring the best and the brightest for their accomplishments in their chosen field and for their contributions and commitment to the African American Community. Next, she is an official member of Forbes The Culture For(bes) The Culture was formed in Boston at the Forbes under 30 Summit in October 2017. They pride themselves on convening current and future Black and Brown leaders worldwide to network, collaborate, share opportunities, and discuss issues related to their communities and the planet at large. She was recognized along with other influential leaders and distinguished entrepreneurs, including Oprah Winfrey, Mel Robbins, Gary V and many more, for the annual Brainz 500 Global Awards List awarded by Brainz Magazine. Lastly, she is a proud member of The Chancellors Round Table at North Carolina A&T State University.

She is a proud member of Delta Sigma Theta Sorority Incorporated, and a member of Alpha Phi Omega. She is very involved in her community, organizations and non-profits. Currently, she is the Co-Founder of Sweetheart Scholars Non-profit Organization 501 (C-3) along with three other powerful women. This scholarship is given out annually to African American Females from her hometown of Wadesboro, North Carolina who are attending college to help with their expenses. Dr. Little believes it takes a village to raise a child and to never forget where you come from. Dr. Little is a strong believer in giving back to her community. She believes our young ladies need vision, direction, and strong mentorship. She is the CEO/Founder/Visionary Author of The ʼ HBCU Experience Movement, LLC the first Black-owned company to launch books written and published by prominent alumni throughout the world who attended Historically Black Colleges & Universities. As authors, they share a powerful collection of stories on how their unique college experience has molded them into the people they are today. Our company's goal is to change the narrative by sharing Black stories and investing financially back into our HBCUs to increase young alumni giving and enrollment. The Award-Winning Best Selling Authors won the Black Authors Matter TV Award May 2021, Inaugural Anthem Awards 2022 and winner of the International Book Awards by The American Book Fest. The books are also apart of the WorldCat.Org the world's largest network of library content and services. Dr. Little is also the Editor and Chief of Creating Your Seat At The Table International Magazine, Advisor for She Wins Society, and Writing and Publishing Coach for the WILDE Winner's Circle.

She is the Founder and Owner of T.A.L.K Radio & TV Network, LLC. Airs in over 167 countries, streamed LIVE on Facebook, YouTube, Twitter and Periscope. Broadcasting and Media Production Company. This live entertainment platform is for new or existing radio shows, television shows, or other electronic media outlets, to air content from a centralized source. All news, information or music shared on this platform are solely the responsibility of the station/radio owner. She is also the Owner and Creator of Creative Broadcasting Radio Station the station of "unlimited possibilities" and Podcast, Radio/TV Host. She is also one of the hosts of the new TV Show Daytime Drama National Syndicated Television Show which will be aired on Comcast Channel 19 and ATT Channel 99 in 19 Middle Tennessee Counties. It will also air on The United Broadcasting Network, The Damascus Roads Broadcasting Network, and Roku. She is CEO/Founder/Visionary Author of The HBCU Experience Movement LLC and CEO/Founder of Little Publishing LLC.

Dr. Little is a 16X Award-Winning Best Selling Author of "Dear Fear, Volume 2 18 Powerful Lessons Of Living Your Best Life Outside Of Fear", "The Gyrlfriend Code Volume 1", "I Survived", "Girl Get Up, and Win", "Glambitious Guide to Being An Entrepreneur", The Price of Greatness, The Making Of A Successful Business Woman, and "Hello Queen". She is a Co-Host for The

Tamie Collins Markee Radio Show, Award-Winning Entrepreneur, Reflection Contributor for the book "NC Girls Living In A Maryland World, Sales/Marketing/Contributing Writer/Event Correspondent for SwagHer Magazine, Contributing Writer for MizCEO Magazine, Contributing Editor for SheIs Magazine, ContributingWriter/ National Sales Executive for Courageous Woman Magazine, Contributing Writer for Upwords International Magazine (India), Contributing Writer/Global Partner for Powerhouse Global International Magazine(London), Host of "Creating Your Seat At The Table", Host of "Authors On The Rise", Co-Host Glambitious Podcast, Partner/Visionary Author of The Gyrlfriend Code The Sorority Edition along with The Gyrlfriend Collective, LLC and CEO/Visionary Author of The HBCU Experience The North Carolina A&T State University Edition. She has been on many different Podcasts, TV Shows, Magazines, and Radio Shows. Lastly, she has received awards such as "Author Of The Month", The Executive Citation of Anne Arundel County, Maryland Award which was awarded by the County Executive Steuart L. Pittman, Top 28 Influential Business Pioneers for K.I.S.H Magazine Spring 2019 Edition. She has been featured in SwagHer Magazine, Power20Magazine Glambitious, Sheen Magazine, All About Inspire Magazine, Formidable Magazine, BRAG Magazine, Sheen Magazine, Front Cover of MizCEO Magazine November 2019, Front Cover for UpWords Magazine October 2019 Edition, Courageous Woman Magazine, Courageous Woman Special Speakers Edition November 2019, Influence Magazine, Featured/Interviewed On a National Syndicated Television Show HBCU 101 on Aspire TV, Dynasty of Dreamers K.I.S.H Magazine Spring 2019 Edition, Dynasty of Dreamers K.I.S.H Magazine September 2019 Edition, Front Cover of Courageous Magazine December 2019, Front Cover of Doz International Magazine January 2020, Top 28 Influential Business Pioneers for K.I.S.H Magazine, Power20 Magazine Glambitious January 2020, Power20 Magazine Glambitious February 2020, Featured in Powerhouse Global International London Magazine March 2020 edition, Featured in

National Boss Magazine October 2020 Edition, Featured in Sheen Magazine February 2020 as one of "The Top 20 Women To Be On The Lookout For In 2020, BlackNews.com, BlackBusiness.com, Front Cover She Speaks Magazine August 2020, Front Cover National Boss Magazine November 2020, BlackNewsScoop.com, Awarded National Women's Empowerment Ministry "Young, Gifted, & Black Award" February 2020 which honors and celebrate women in business such as Senior Level Executives, Entrepreneurs and CEO's below age 40 for their creativity and business development. Featured in National Women Empowerment Magazine 2020, Featured in Black Enterprise 2020, Featured on Fox, NBC, CBS 2020, Featured/Interviewed on National Syndicated Television The Black Report on Fox Soul TV, Front Cover for National Boss Magazine 2020, Speaker at The Black College Expo 2020, Speaker for Creative CEO's summit January 2021, International Speaker for Living Your Dream Life Summit 2021, Speaker for Elite Business Women Powershift Conference 2021, Keynote Speaker/Host/Panelist for The Bella, The Brand & Her Bag Wealth Summit 2021, Speaker for The Unstoppable You Summit January 2021, Speaker for Marketing Mastery Summit for Glambitious 2021, Speaker for Crown Yourself Conference January 2021, Featured in Sheen Print Magazine 2021, Speaker at Door Dash Virtual Black History Month Celebration, Speaker for Day Of Aggie Generations with North Carolina A&T State University, 2021 Woman of Black Excellence Honoree, Guest/Speaker on podcast The Happy Hour Show, Speaker for the Phoenix Jack & Jill HBCU Author Showcase, Guest/Speaker on The JMosley Show, Contributing Author for "Prayers For The Entrepreneurial Woman Book", Speaker for Creative Con, Recognized as one of Today's Black History Makers, Speaker at From Paper to Profits conference, Press Conference/Press for "Don't Waste Your Petty" Movie, Press Conference/Press for Mahalia Jackson movie, Speaker for HerStory Women's Global Empowerment Summit, Speaker for HerStory Women Who Lead Conference, Speaker for Stepping N2 Sisterhood Sharing Winning Secrets Virtual Summit, Speaker for I AM Glambitious Virtual

Conference, Speaker for Black Authors Matter TV show, Speaker for Thought Leaders Global Virtual Summit, Speaker for A Conversation with Floyd Marshall Jr., Black Authors Matter TV Award Winner, Speaker for Sheen Talk, Foreword Author for the anthology "It Cost To Be The Boss", Top 50 Most Influential Women recognized by VIP Global Magazine, Speaker at Black Writers Weekend, Speaker on The GameChangers With Angela Ward Show Keynote Speaker for Blacks In Nonprofits Conference, Speaker for Leap Conference, Speaker on Pass The Mic Sis, Speaker for From Purpose to Profit Summit, Speaker on The Been Worthy Podcast, Speaker/Host for The Miz CEO Graduation, Featured in Emoir Magazine for Building A Global Media Empire, Making Black History Today recipient for Glambitious, She's Making Women's History Today recipient for Glambitious and TEDx Host as well to name a few.

Dr. Little received her undergraduate degree in English from North Carolina A&T State University. Next, she received her Master's Degree in Industrial Organizational Psychology. She has received her Doctorate in Leadership as well. Dr. Little is a mover and shaker and she continuously pushes herself to be better than she was yesterday. She gives GOD all the credit for everything that has happened in her life. She has strong faith and determination to be great. She believes her only competition is herself. Her favorite scripture is Philippians 4:13 "I can do all things through Christ who strengthens me".

Table of Contents

continued...

LARRY J. ALLEN

Foreword
Larry J. Allen

Historically Black Colleges and Universities (HBCUs) are the mecca of Black excellence, immersing ourselves in our culture through bands, Greek and social fellowships, community service, and multiple student-led organizations. HBCUs were created to provide education without racial discrimination for students of color. Founders, such as William H. Holland, founded these notable institutions to provide educational outlets for people of color to be successful. The purpose of these institutions has been fulfilled to date as we see the excellence that hails from HBCUs.

As a senior in high school, college was the last thing on my mind. As a young adolescent attending music academies for grade school, such as Garden Villas Music Academy and Meyerland Performing & Visual Arts, formerly known as Johnston Middle School, I knew exactly what I wanted to do with my life. College initially was an afterthought. I performed professionally early on in life and the various schools I attended prepared me for a career in the entertainment industry. Even at such a young age, I knew I would be exactly where I am today in my career.

I applied to a lot of universities (seemed like the thing to do as senior), HBCUs as well as D1 institutions. I was accepted to all of them while being offered full scholarships to attend. It wasn't until I attended the Labor Day Classic in Houston, Texas that I made the decision to go to college. After seeing the Marching Storm, the drum majors, and the percussion section (PVMcFunkBOX), I knew I was going to be a Panther. I knew I was going to be in the band, as well as become drum major. That was the goal. That was the plan. I wasn't going to accept or settle for anything less.

As I arrived on "The Hill", I felt the vibes of campus life, classes, fraternities and sororities, the beautiful women, marching band and parties (not too many), creating a lifetime of memories with friends that I probably wouldn't have met if it wasn't for Prairie View. My professional career has been an ode to the HBCU experience, even more so to Prairie View A&M University. As the university's motto states, "PV produces productive people!" I am truly the definition of this motto! After obtaining my Master's degree in Sociology, as well as my Bachelor's degree in Music, attending Prairie View set me up with the tools to be highly productive and successful in the field of music and entertainment, where the competition is extremely competitive and cutthroat.

During the end-of-the-year band banquet, the guest speaker asked us, "Who knows where they're going to be in the next five to eight years?" I raised my hand and he asked what my plan was. I confidently told him I'll be a Grammy Award- winning musician and perform for people all over the world. *I did just that!* I won a Grammy as a recording musician for work on the film *Homecoming* by Beyonce and living abroad performing in various countries across Asia and Europe.

Home band videos turned into movie appearances on VH1, Netflix and MTV. The Cotton Bowl turned into Coachella (Beyonce). Music major seminars turned into performances on the American Music Award stage, and the list goes on. I remember spamming my professors with my music and creative ideas. They would always say, "You remind me of Quincy Jones. Hollywood's calling your name. Go make us proud!" I've been fortunate enough to give back to my alma mater via various charitable events, as well as casting current and former students for film appearances, major TV network performances, and studio recordings for some of the biggest artists to date. I can honestly say I fully enjoyed the HBCU experience at my alma mater and I don't regret any of the memories made at Prairie View because it helped me become the man I am today.

As the Marching Storm says, "We are the Marching Storm. We abide by our creed. We're all we got! We're all we need!"

P... V... UUUUU KKKKNNNNOOOOOWWWWW!

#RIH Professor Edwards

About Larry J. Allen

Grammy Award Winner-Recording Artist-Singer/Songwriter-Music Producer-Choreographer- Creative Director

Larry J. Allen, also known as *LA* or *YOU.C.LA* is an American music producer, performer, singer/songwriter, and choreographer from Houston Texas. At the tender age of three, LA's Mother and Father notice music would be the foundation of his life. Getting lost in a local mall in Houston, LA was found unharmed in the Brook Mays Piano store plunking on the keys and from the crowd that gathered around to watch a baby attempt to play was breath taken. Immediately LA's parents enrolled him in every music program allowed along with sending him to Garden Villas Music Academy for schooling and further training. While in school LA started out on violin and was quickly recruited by head Director of Bands Carrol Cummings and auditioned LA on percussion but soon realized he had the ability to play multiple instruments telling his parents "Little Larry wants to play everything, he has a GOD given talent so I'm going to let him explore his musical abilities" -Carrol Cummings

By Middle School LA was proficient on all Brass and Percussion instruments as well as Clarinet(self-taught) and then was introduced to the Ross Shaw Sterling Raider Marching Band and instantly fell in love. LA excelled highly in grade school and was offered a full scholarship on any brass or percussion instrument from the late great Professor George Edwards at Prairie View A&M University which he accepted, turning down similar offers from various other HBCU's and Division 1 schools.

While at PVAMU, LA continued to progress in music becoming Drum Major just after his first year and ultimately becoming Head Drum Major in the years that followed. After graduating with a B.A.

in Music (percussion) LA was hired on as Graduate Assistant of bands and worked part time as Lead Trumpeter for the NFL's Houston Texans Pep Band soon after graduating with a Master of Arts degree in Sociology (PVAMU). While on staff at PVAMU in 2010, Dr. Nicholas Thomas (Asst. Director of Bands FAMU) placed a call to Don P. Roberts about a guy in Texas that would be great for the Theatrical Production DRUMline Live.

After a brief audition LA was offered two parts in the show. Trumpet and Percussion and just like in school LA took the new opportunity and expanded on it and just the next year LA was hired to be on the creative staff for DRUMline Live as well as Assistant Percussion Director and cast member. While working with DRUMline Live, LA began to write and produce songs in multiple genres of music for artists around Texas and California. LA was also commissioned by Universal Studios Japan where he lived for over a year and while in Japan LA created a buzz for his own music and started to record an album soon after releasing the Good Vibes album worldwide.

LA was also a part of the Guinness Book of World Records (HtxCyper) on July 18, 2015 for most solo vocals performed in one song (315). LA has also produced tracks for the Google convention and also produced and performed for H&M clothing during fashion week in New York City. From being the Percussion Director for Beyoncé's historical Coachella performance, as well as receiving Grammy accolades for participating as a recording musician on Beyoncé's Homecoming: The Live Album, American Music Award performances with Ciara & Missy Elliott, performances on Ellen, HBO, Netflix, and producing for films such as A Family Hip Hop Christmas (VH1/MTV) Little, Marvel, and Nickelodeon they're two words to describe LA… as the Director and CEO of DRUMline Live Don P. Roberts puts it, "LA's a **Natural Performer**"!

KAYLA ROBINSON

Becoming a Productive Panther
Kayla Robinson

"[*Prairie View*] taught me the meaning of womanhood and my place as a black woman in this world. I graduated with a degree in confidence, self-esteem, perseverance & determination."
–Mo Ivory

As a young girl, I always dreamed of attending a Historically Black College or University (HBCU), but Prairie View A&M University was not originally on my list of colleges or universities. By my senior year of high school, my perspective shifted drastically and I only wanted to attend Louisiana State University as this was the school of choice in my family. I applied to three schools towards the end of my junior year: LSU, Texas Southern University, and Prairie View A&M University. Prairie View made the list because at that time I was interested in exploring a career path in Juvenile Forensic Psychology–PV was one of the few universities with this program. So with strong encouragement from my mother, I applied.

After submitting my application, I received my acceptance letter. I also received an additional letter shortly after. The second letter invited me to the school's 2011 Homecoming festivities with the opportunity of possibly qualifying for a scholarship. Not knowing what was in store for me, my mother and I decided to see what PV had to offer. This was not only my first-time visiting Prairie View A&M University, but also my first time visiting the state of Texas.

Once I stepped foot on the campus on November 19, 2011, I immediately fell in love. I knew then Prairie View A&M University was for me and would soon become my new home the following year. At the end of the scholarship presentation, I was unexpectedly awarded the Regents' Student Merit Scholarship and I accepted. This is an academic based scholarship that waived out of state fees which was huge for me because I'm from the Chicago Area. I was elated! That same day, I went on a tour of the campus and experienced campus life at its peak due to it being homecoming weekend.

Coming back to Prairie View in the fall of 2012 was going to be a little different as my parents moved me into University College–Building 37. I had a range of emotions because I knew I would not go back home until the holiday break. I was so scared, yet so excited. I didn't know anyone who attended PV nor anyone in the state of Texas and little did I know, at that time, there were other classmates with similar feelings. However, Panther Camp allowed me to meet people, begin building my network, and get accustomed to campus life. Panther Camp was a week where only incoming freshmen were on campus with a few upperclassmen who we called Panther Advisory Leaders (PALS). Adjusting to college life took some time, but I was able to remain disciplined and maintain my focus on academics.

The second semester of my freshman year, I was enrolled in College Algebra. The professor pulled me aside to ask me some questions regarding my major as I was excelling in this course and tutoring my classmates. I was a double major in Criminal Justice and Psychology, again Juvenile Forensic Psychology was the end goal. It was from this conversation that I saw first-hand the professors "at The University" cared greatly about their students. The following semester, I changed my major from Criminal Justice and Psychology to Chemical Engineering. The course load in the College of Engineering was much more intense and challenged me to work to my full potential. The professors ensured that I took advantage of *every* opportunity.

During the summer of 2014, I was accepted into an Undergraduate Research Program at Massachusetts Institute of Technology (MIT), in Boston, Massachusetts, where I interfaced with college students from Ivy League schools. Not only was I the only one from Prairie View A&M University and other HBCUs, I was the only African American in this program. This was my first experience being the only one, that looked like me, in the room and it prepared me for my career.

I later became a recipient of the Shell Incentive Fund Scholarship from Shell Oil Company. After receiving this scholarship, I was officially being paid to go to school. I continued to work and saved the money from Shell to use once I finished at PV. This money was used to fund my master's degree from the University of Louisville– I always liked to plan ahead.

It was at Prairie View that I discovered my passion for traveling. I studied abroad with the College of Engineering in Jinan, Shandong, China, where I took Introduction to Electrical Engineering at the University of Jinan the summer of 2015. This experience was like no other and one I don't regret. I was exposed to Chinese culture and learned to speak a little Mandarin. Later, I was invited by the School of Architecture to join on a service-learning trip to Puerto Rico. While on this trip, we worked with residents to develop and implement sustainable eco-friendly solutions along with rebuilding play areas for children. Both experiences were eye opening and increased my appreciation of the small things we tend to take for granted.

I traveled with the University to Washington, D.C., to witness the opening of the African American Smithsonian Museum where President Barack Obama led the opening ceremony in September 2016. This was a once in a lifetime experience!

My college experience was more than just academics. I became heavily involved in campus life by initially joining the PV Choice Committee 2012-2013. This opportunity exposed me to the endless possibilities Prairie View had to offer! From there I didn't stop. I became a member of the following: Student Government Association-Senator and 2016-2017 Executive Vice President, National Society of Collegiate Scholars-Treasurer, Tau Beta Pi Honor Society, Omega Chi Epsilon Honor Society, National Society of

Black Engineers-Treasurer, Panther Advisor Leaders (PALS), along with a plethora of other organizations and campus activities. And yes, I attended a multitude of parties both on and off campus including the notorious Tent Party. I also participated in Hump Day every Wednesday.

Becoming SGA Executive Vice President was humbling and presented its own challenges. During my term as Vice President there were both highs and lows. A high that will forever impact the trajectory of Prairie View A&M University was the opening of the New Panther Stadium in the fall of 2016. This allowed the University to enhance recruitment of the best talents given the substantial upgrade in amenities. Student enrollment also increased drastically during this time as some students were housed in hotels in Cypress due to lack of on-campus housing.

While serving as Vice President for SGA, I was able to meet with administration to start the discussion around the use of the stadium as it pertained to graduation. Prior to the opening of the stadium, graduation tickets were issued and the number of tickets issued per person was based on the size of the graduating class. Within our culture there are students who will become first-generation graduates and it was uncomfortable for them to select which family member should attend graduation. The new stadium later eliminated this obstacle for students.

Not only was I exposed to Prairie View A&M University's President and Cabinet, I was also exposed at a higher level to the Secretary of State, Chancellors of the Texas A&M System, and worked directly with the Student Regent. I met with other student leaders from schools on the A&M System in Austin, Texas, to discuss issues that were being experienced on campus in search of resolutions.

Learning to navigate through adversity was key during my tenure at Prairie View. Here is where I learned that diversity in cultures, political awareness, influential leadership, and difference in perspective allows for navigation of life experiences. There were several times where it would have been easy to give up; however, with the support of my family and the vast resources of my PV family, I persevered.

I graduated *magna cum laude* with a Bachelor of Science in Chemical Engineering with a concentration in Bioengineering. I can honestly say my experience at Prairie View A&M University is one that I will forever cherish. PV embellished on my confidence to walk into any room and create a seat for myself at any table. Overall, the experience helps you recognize you're not in the fight alone once you leave the city of Prairie View and enter the world. I've not only gained lifelong friends but a reliable network. There is always a 'Productive Panther' somewhere who has your back and willing to lend a listening ear, the network is impeccable. When you mention that you graduated from Prairie View A&M University, the world knows your capabilities and no obstacle is too large for you to conquer.

About Kayla Robinson

Kayla Raynelle Robinson is a native of the Chicagoland Area and the third of four children. She has two brothers and one sister. She attended Marian Catholic High School in Chicago Heights, Illinois, graduating in the top ten percentile of her class. She is a proud 2017 graduate of Prairie View A&M University in Prairie View, Texas, where she obtained her Bachelor of Science in Chemical Engineering with a concentration in Bioengineering. Kayla furthered her education by continuing onto graduate school at the University of Louisville in Louisville, Kentucky. Here she completed her Masters of Engineering in Engineering Management (MEM) in 2018. Kayla currently lives in Baton Rouge, Louisiana, where she is an Engineer for one of the largest chemical companies worldwide. Kayla has always been heavily involved in volunteering and giving back to the community as she actively participates in a wide-range of public service activities while sustaining a full-time working career. Kayla is a strong advocate for increasing minority interest and involvement in Science, Technology, Engineering, and Math (STEM). She participates in events within her community by engaging with the youth to introduce them to the opportunities the STEM field has to offer. Kayla is a proud member of the Illustrious Sisterhood of Delta Sigma Theta Sorority, Inc. and serves on several committees. She is a lifetime member of the Prairie View A&M University National Alumni Association. Kayla is also a member of the Junior League of Baton Rouge making an impact on her community by working with a diverse group of women. In her spare time, Kayla enjoys spending time with friends and family. She is an active traveler both domestic and international. And when it's football season, Kayla attends the New Orleans Saints home games as she is a season ticket holder.

ALARIC JONES

The 290 HBCU Experience
Alaric Jones

The HBCU experience is an integral part of my life. Each component of the HBCU experience has played an important part in my maturation. Growing up with parents and grandparents who are HBCU graduates, it is hard to shy away from how they have blessed me throughout my life.

My HBCU experience starts with myself being a third-generation graduate from Southern University and A&M College. With my family being die hard Jaguars, I didn't realize that my HBCU experience would lead me down Highway 290 to Prairie View A&M University. As a sophomore chemistry major and future chemical engineer, I was able to intern with Shell Oil Company in Houston, Texas. Here I was able to not only gain hands on work experience, but I was also able to network with other interns who looked like me. The interns who I had grown close to were Prairie View students. As chemical engineering students, they spoke on the good things about the program at PV like the course work, the teachers, and the career opportunities. I was very intrigued by the information I learned about PV and its chemical engineering program. This would essentially be my first conversation and hearings about the school down 290.

My goal in college was to become a chemical engineer. Since my undergraduate institution did not have this major, my department head advised me to go to grad school. I had looked at several institutions for graduate school like MIT, UCLA, and Texas A&M. Then I remembered the conversations I had about Prairie View during my internship. These conversations that I didn't think much of at the time, led me to attending graduate school at PV.

The graduate courses at Prairie View were detailed and rigorous. I felt like I was equipped with the tools to succeed in the work force. My favorite professor was Dr. Sheena Reeves, whom most people would say was the toughest professor in the department. Despite being a difficult professor, Dr. Reeves provided her students with the knowledge necessary for us to be great in the class. She also taught my favorite class, which was separation process engineering. This class centered on separating compounds into their purest form through separation processes such as distillation. One reason why separation process engineering was one of my favorites is because my professor taught this course very well. I was able to grasp the concepts. Another reason this was my favorite class is because the information I obtained in this class was essential to working effectively in a plant as a chemical engineer. I utilize the concepts learned in this class every day at my job.

With Prairie View being so close to Houston, it is close to some of the biggest companies in the world that hire engineers. In fact, one of the biggest reasons why I came to PV was due to its proximity to the oil capitol of the world in Houston. The schools host a very large and diverse career fair where students can network with companies of their choice. I was blessed to be a part of the career fair as a student and as a recruiter. As a student, I was able to secure an internship with Monsanto (now Bayer) as a research chemical engineering intern in St. Louis, Missouri. I was able to use the chemical engineering and chemistry tools I've learned at PV and SU on the job. As a recruiter, I had the opportunity to speak with students on their career aspirations, give resume tips, and even offer them internship opportunities.

Today, I work as a process engineer at Shell Oil Company in Houston, Texas. Here I support the conversion of crude oil out of the ground into refined gasoline that we use in our cars, planes, and trains today. From reaction chemistry to separation processes to material balances, all of these classes have prepared me to become successful on the job. Along with the basic skills needed to function within my job requirements, attending Prairie View also allowed me to learn communication skills and become successful at public speaking. The technical and soft skills are essential when working with those who come from some of the top schools in the country.

My last year at PV, I was able to secure a graduate assistant position in the Athletic Department. This was probably one of the highlights during my time at PV. In this role, I assisted student athletes with their schoolwork and kept track of their study hall hours needed to stay eligible. Because I love sports, the opportunity to help student athletes was amazing. I was able to help from all over the world in a plethora of sports. As a graduate assistant, I noticed how difficult it can be for a student to balance athletics and school simultaneously. However, I think the school did an amazing job of giving the student athletes the tools needed to succeed and to help them balance their workload.

My time at Prairie View A&M University was short and sweet. It gave me the opportunity to experience another HBCU and obtain the knowledge needed to be successful in my career. Not only am I successful, but I am able to compete with my peers from other top universities. I am forever grateful to continue in the same vein as my parents and grandparents as a HBCU alum.

About Alaric Jones

Alaric hails from the great city of Alexandria, Louisiana where he attended Peabody Magnet High School. He is a graduate of Southern University and A&M College, in Baton Rouge, Louisiana, where he received his B.S. in Chemistry. He also received his M.S. in Chemical Engineering from Prairie View A&M University, in Praire View, Texas.

Alaric currently lives in the city of Houston, TX, where he works as Process Engineer in the oil and gas industry. He was initiated into the Beta Sigma Chapter of Omega Psi Phi Fraternity, Inc. at Southern University. In his fraternity, he held the position of International Undergraduate Representative to the Supreme Council. He gives back in the city of Houston by helping increase the participation of African American youth in the sport of baseball by mentoring and hosting camps. Along with sports, he also volunteers to help promote STEM (Science, Technology, Engineering, and Math) among African American youth. Alaric loves to watch sports and is an avid HBCU and Saints fan!"

CHASMIN JENKINS

Legends Leave Legacy
Chasmin Jenkins

To leave a legacy means to put a stamp on the future. To contribute something that may be valued for generations to come. Kobe Bryant once said, "Leave the game better than you found it; and when it comes time for you to leave the game, leave a legend." I would like to think that my experience at PVAMU was legendary. More importantly, I would like to think that I left PV as a legend.

Now I don't say that with a sense of ego; nor is it with any sense of cockiness. I say that with a sense of pride. A sense of pride in my alma mater for who she shaped me to be. A sense of pride for the *memories dear; for friends and recollections*. I truly take a sense of pride in the legend that *is* PVAMU. In the legend that it raised, and for the traditions and legacy that has been going strong for 146 years and counting.

See, it isn't just me that left PV a legend; we all did. Whether we were involved in student organizations or *The Marching Storm*, or played a sport, lived off campus, participated in Greek Life, threw parties, or simply just went to class and back to your room, we can all think back to some moment where we felt like a legend on that yard. PV just does that to you. It embraces you and grows you. It empowers you to *want* to be a part of something greater than yourself. PV brings out the legend in you.

So many students, like myself, go off to college alone. They're excited and hopeful, but they have no true understanding of what they are going to experience over the next few years of life. They may have a few preconceived notions based off nineties sitcoms, movies, and old college stories from older friends and family. This was my case. To be perfectly transparent, it was the reason that I *did not* want to attend PV originally.

I grew up an only child of the most amazing and outstanding parents anybody could ever pray for (literally)! While these two didn't meet on the yard, the yard is where they fell in love. While this is (obviously) shaping up to be a beautiful testament of PV love, understand that this meant that my entire childhood, I was engulfed in PVAMU. I grew up listening to the *memories dear* of people like them, my aunt and uncle, my godfather, my big cousin, my great aunt, and my Grammy (great-grandmother). I just wanted something *different*! So, I thought.

I grew up attending *The State Fair Classic*, where we always went to visit the late, and so great, Prof Edwards, who was deemed my godfather during the days of my daddy marching as his head-drum major, and my mama being thrown in the air on the sideline as a cheerleader. I grew up going to events and galas hosted by the *Prairie View National Alumni Association – Fort Worth Chapter* and hearing stories of how my daddy used to pull out his turntables and crates to deejay in front of Holly Hall. He'd turn an ordinary day into a party.

I grew up surrounded by these things; yet, I also experienced a polar opposite world. I loved school growing up, and I was very attentive to my studies. I held several leadership roles in student organizations and had great relationships with friends and teachers— all while often being the only brown-skinned girl in the room (and sometimes on the team). College fairs and college tours weren't exactly highlighting Historically Black Colleges and Universities (HBCUs) in my area; and the high schools (as you can assume) were not promoting them either.

While I was most certainly *attracted* to Prairie View, my seventeen-year-old self thought I needed to be with my high school friends. Above all, I had to be different than everybody else in my family! What I didn't understand then is that my family had already set the precedence of legacy and having legendary experiences on The Hill. While I thought I wanted my norm of an environment to stay the same in college, what I couldn't see then is how shaking up my norm is the very thing that shaped the legacy I am now a part of, as well as the legacy I am now creating.

Then, I got there.

Freshmen move-in day was lit! I was sold! I walked in the UC, bright-eyed and bushy-tailed with suitcases on top of boxes on top of trunks on top of crates with my teary-eyed, but excited, parents. I followed the map to find Building 41 and meet up with my roommate, Evan Elizabeth, who I had already met and deemed my new bestie four months prior at cheer tryouts and cheer practices! We moved in and got our spaces as chic as can be and *quickly* hugged our parents before sending them down 290! It was time for the Courtyard Party, baby! This was our first introduction to the legend that is PVAMU.

The weeks to follow were unforgettable as we went to Panther Camp and got acclimated and acquainted with the Building 41 Cover girls and overall college life. We quickly learned the student-athlete balance as we hopped on a bus to Orlando the first week of class for the SWAC vs MEAC Championship. It was our first game. We explored Disneyworld with PV Cheer and PV Football. We lost that game but being exposed to such an experience so early helped me to set goals and really aspire to be somebody at PV.

I returned to campus with a fire to get involved. I made fast friends in the MSC and at UC Football and talked to my PALS about being more active. Before I knew it, I was in meetings every day, paying for t-shirts once a week, and working with campus staff. I was running around like a chicken with its head cut off if I'm being honest. However, I was making an impact. I was now listening to the advice of the legends before me and adding to that to create my own legacy. I stayed active in student organizations the rest of freshman year, while creating the most legendary memories, squeezing in the blue Honda with my girls Evan, Dominique, Ikia, Shonte, Kiona and Aivaye! We were inseparable!

The years to come only got greater as I got more involved and as I really grew into Chasmin. Sophomore year, I moved off campus to Brookside. By then, I had a lil street cred. I'm super social by nature and will talk to a wall. By now, I had quite a few friends in various social circles. This meant Fuentes Happy Hours and Brookside Kickbacks were always *the move*. Not to mention legendary parties like the Tent Party, Toga VII by the Kappas, and KKPsi's Foam Party in Houston. You know we *had* to be there if DJ Chose was in the mix! I worked alongside party promotion groups like Get Mon-E and Just Jeff and lived in the moment of being a young college student.

Sounds like I partied a lot, huh? And did! But I was still doing my job. I became a member of PALS and mentored freshmen. I joined SGA and worked on the student committee responsible for "the passage of the student referendum which allowed [the] vision to come to fruition" for what is now known as Panther Stadium. I was accepted into Kappa Delta Pi International Honor Society for Education, ran for homecoming court, and pledged the smooth and dominant *Omega Gamma Chapter of Zeta Phi Beta Sorority, Inc.*, the finest sorority in the land. Even this was legacy. I joined a sorority that had such a rich legacy of sisterhood, service, scholarship, and finer womanhood. I joined a chapter that was an important catalyst to the PVAMU campus, as the first Greek letter organization on The Yard (check the archives, boo), as well as a new type of bond with my Delta Theta dad (Phi Beta Sigma Fraternity, Inc.)

Greek Life was a whole new world. Bonding with my line sisters (the "livest line to touch dine," SPR13 - *12 Unbroken SecretzZ*), my prophytes, and our dean, LaDonna gave me a lifelong bond and sisterhood that I will always cherish. My line sisters and I are still remarkably close today and support each other tremendously. I'm the godmother to the sweetest, most amazing little girl, Riyan, who is actually my dean's daughter. Zeta gave me, an only child, sisters that have my back when there's not a party going on and who I can call when I need to vent. The work we put in on our yard and in the Prairie View community is still making an impact. Today, we are each thriving in and creating our own paths. Liiiiinsthithas! I love you. I'm proud of every single one of you. ~ACE (First On.)

Junior year, I moved back onto campus to become a community assistant (CA) in University College (UC), our freshman housing community. I was a CA for Building 40 Divas. For the first time, I had the chance to really do what I wanted in terms of creating programs and events for my residents. I had the best boss and teammate, Oliver and Heavener. We worked to create an environment where our freshmen residents felt accepted, affirmed and empowered about who they are as women and the greatness they possess. We pushed our residents to find the things that make them happy and to chase their dreams. Led by Mr. Jackson and Ms. Barker, the UC staff was a family that genuinely wanted our residents to succeed. Legends like them trained and cultivated a UC Family of Legends like me, Veazie, Washington, Mayhorn and Daniels. From those seeds, an extensive line of legends is currently making this impact even greater as they continue this legacy.

Prairie View opened doors for me that may not have opened had I chose to go elsewhere. On January 19, 2013, I boarded a private-chartered, double-decker airplane to Washington, D.C. to attend the inauguration of President Barack Obama. The entire trip was the experience of a lifetime. Yet, it was one of many instances where PV engulfed us in the celebration of who we were as young Black people and who we could become.

Junior year wrapped up with a bang as I competed in the 45th Annual Miss Prairie View A&M University Scholarship Pageant. I, again, made fast sisters with a dynamic group of women, who had each made such a tremendous impact on our campus and had ambitious plans on how to make this impact even greater. Each of these women inspired me then and they inspire me now. They are each diversifying their impact to reach more people and change more lives. Whether you won or not, you left a legacy that is still felt today.

Summer came fast and my final semester came even faster. I was approved to begin student teaching in the fall and set to graduate in December. I lived in Cypress and was commuting to Waller. Senior semester was very calm and came with a lot of lessons. Senior year made me slow down and adjust to a new norm of life. I was doing the full-time, live-in boyfriend, with jobs thing. It was the first time I had a real taste of adult life. Life changed fast as I adjusted from an on-campus, student-athlete-organization, party girl to a fourth-grade math/science teacher, then to a kindergarten teacher. I grew up. I adjusted. I recognized that the legend that I had been on campus now had to become legacy so I could be legendary in a new stage of my life.

There is a time and a season for everything. A time to plant seeds, and a time to reap the harvest. Throughout my three and a half years on The Hill, I experienced joy. I experienced pain. I experienced hardships and heartbreaks. I grew. I studied. I excelled. I partied. I had a little bit of everything. My journey was *my* journey. I owned it. I made sure that I did legendary things while I was there. I made the game better than I found it. And when my time was up, I packed up the lessons from those games, used them to propel me into my next season, and left a legend. I had to trust that the seeds that I planted then were going to grow for generations to come, thus creating my legacy.

Prairie View produces productive people. That statement alone speaks to the legacy that is PVAMU and the generations of legends that have come down University Drive. Today, my closest friends are some of the same people mentioned in this reflection, and we often discuss how PV truly shaped us into who we are today. The seeds and relationships that were planted on the yard have sprouted into phenomenal businesses, partnerships, successful teachers, and, most importantly, confidence in going for whatever it is that you dream of. PV gave us that. I look at friends like Scooby, Brandi, Gee, Monica, Jazzi, Desmun, 4.0, Kiki, Trah, Gary, Kewi, Deidre, JT, Kevin, and so many more who are each creating their own lane and walking in the dreams that we talked about between beer pong games. They decided to cultivate those seeds and become legendary.

Whether you were named or not,
Whether you had a family of legends before you or not,
Whether you even went to PV or not…

You can be legendary in your own right. Every person who goes down University Drive will have a legendary experience because Prairie View A&M University *is* legendary. Every person that goes down (<u>your name</u>) Drive will have a (<u>that's for you to decide</u>) experience because (<u>your name</u>) is (<u>again, that's for you to decide</u>).

What kind of experience are you creating for people and how are you cultivating seeds of legacy in your own life and journey? How are you embracing the legacy that you have already left? Legends surround themselves with legends. I see you, legend.

Do you?

"Give to the world the best you have."

~Most Honorable Arizona Cleaver Stemmons,
Founder, Zeta Phi Beta Sorority, Inc.

About Chasmin Jenkins

Chasmin arrived at THE Prairie View A&M University in August 2011. From the moment she arrived on The Yard, she became highly engaged in campus and social activities, which predicted her trajectory of success and legacy on The Hill.

Chasmin was a member of various student organizations including Cheerleading and SGA. While being highly engaged on campus and working hard to leave a legacy, Chasmin was able to maintain a 3.5 GPA ranking her amongst the top of her class. Chasmin became a member of THE Omega Gamma chapter of Zeta Phi Beta Sorority, Inc in Spring 2013, where she served in many capacities. Other involvement includes Panther Advisory Leaders (PALS), Community Assistant for freshman housing, and even a run for Miss Prairie View.

After graduating with a Bachelor of Science in Interdisciplinary Studies in December 2014, Chasmin moved back to her hometown of Arlington, TX where she began her career in education. After a successful career as a teacher, head cheerleading coach, and assistant principal, Chasmin has since transitioned into entrepreneurship and is the proud owner *of cJenk the Agency: Creative Concierge, LLC* and *Raggedi Luxury Durags* in Dallas, TX.

Chasmin has a passion for engagement, growth, and connecting people. These keep her motivated and driven to not only positively impact the world around her, but to leave a lasting legacy.

KIERRA S. JONES

Transformation

Kierra S. Jones

For many people, college is where they find themselves. Others feel like college builds on a preexisting foundation. For myself, Prairie View changed the way I thought and approached everything in my life. It began the day I made that life-changing decision.

The Decision (2011-2012)

Sometimes, it all comes down to that one decision, one day, or one second that can change everything forever. I will never forget the day when I discovered that I wanted to become a PVAMU Black Panther. I was a senior in high school when I attended a college fair held in my hometown. I walked into the huge convention center, feeling completely overwhelmed by all the different types of school representatives' booths. Where most students and parents walked around with excitement looking for the perfect college, I, on the other hand, was completely lost and filled with anxiety. I went to every single booth one by one, grabbing every brochure that each school had to offer. The very last booth was Prairie View A&M University. With a handful of brochures, I approached the booth.

"You won't need all those brochures once you hear about PV, young lady!" I was greeted by the most enthusiastic recruiter I had met all day. I came home screaming and waving two purple and gold pom-poms given to me by the recruiter as a promise that I would attend PV (I still have those pom-poms today, in hopes of one day passing them to my children). I couldn't wait to tell my mom that I found the college of my dreams. That same night, my childhood best friend, who also became my freshman roommate, and I stayed up all night attempting to learn all the previous PV shuffles on YouTube. Our minds were sold on the idea of becoming Panthers and we were in awe of the culture. To honor the wishes of my school counselor and mother, I applied to other schools; however, I never opened any of the letters until my Prairie View acceptance letter arrived.

The Experience (2013-2017)

Even a caterpillar must crawl in the dirt before it can soar as a butterfly. I think of each year at PVAMU as a step in a *metamorphosis*, a Greek word that means *transformation*. The four stages of the monarch butterfly's life cycle are the egg, the larvae (caterpillar), the pupa (chrysalis), and the adult butterfly. The four generations are actually four different butterflies going through these four stages for one year until it is time to start over again.

Freshman Year: The Egg Stage

It was officially freshman move-in day on "The Hill," and I was filled with excitement. It was like a scene from a movie. Turning into the University College also known as the "UC," we were welcomed with the sweet sounds of the Marching Storm drum line. Various members of the campus Greek life helped with carrying boxes and drove golf carts transporting families to and from the parking lot. Families took proud pictures of their children. I took a deep breath. *Wow, this is really my home for the next four years*. Building 39 ("TRE NINE"), second floor, room 219, side B was not just a dorm room; it was truly a home.

My fondest memories of freshman year were the 5:00 a.m. wake-up calls from our PALS during Panther Camp, hanging out in the first floor "TV room," naps in between classes, campus-sponsored events, Hump Day, Club MSC during Catfish Friday, long walks to "Hobart Texas," threats of $150 fines if you walked on the grass (due to the rich history), spending all my Panther bucks too early in the semester, and college parties. Trying to balance classes and my work-study job on campus wasn't easy. I prided myself on never missing anything PV had to offer; but oftentimes, my classes got the least attention. With the guidance and support of upperclassmen ladies on campus who I admired as role models, they were able to teach me about balance and set a great example of what a PVAMU woman truly means in and outside the classroom.

Sophomore Year- The Larvae (Caterpillar)

Entering my sophomore year, I knew that I needed to make some significant changes from the previous year and focus highly on academics. After being undecided, I officially selected to pursue my degree from the Marvin D. and June Samuel Brailsford College of Arts and Sciences as a pre-dental candidate. Now that I was in my course classes, I had no choice but to buckle down and focus on my studies. I spent most of my time studying either in my room, at Jazzman's Bakery & Café in the John B. Coleman Library with a strawberry banana smoothie or did all-nighters in room A101 in the Biology Department. The program was rigorous yet, the faculty and staff were always available for help. The Biology Department helped me grow out of my comfort zone, push past my insecurities, developed my public speaking persona and professional dress.

Junior Year- The Pupa (Chrysalis)

Making an everlasting legacy at Prairie View was an important pillar for me. Prairie View has a magnitude of student life organizations that can cater to anyone's personality or interest. Junior year, I joined and held leadership positions in a host of student life organizations: Student Government Association (SGA), Panther Advisors Leaders (PALS), PVAMU Partnership and Outreach, Sigma Xi National Honor Society, and National Model United Nations. I also was the co-founder of a new organization on campus. Be The Match is a global leader in bone marrow transplantation and connects patients with their donor match for a life-saving marrow or blood stem cell. Be The Match is an organization that still remains on the campus to this day and continues to save and touch lives. Joining student organizations at PV presented many opportunities to learn more about myself, my goals, and my strength. It taught me multitasking and organizational skills, as well as how to generate ideas and serve others. These self-awareness skills became beneficial in my current career.

Senior Year – The Butterfly

During my graduate matriculation, I worked as a research student assistant under the leadership of Dr. Yolander Youngblood as the lead researcher. I presented my research in a multitude of symposiums. That same semester, I became a member of the Eta Beta Chapter of Delta Sigma Theta Sorority, Incorporated, where I served as the collegiate member of the Regional Nominating Committee for the Southwest Region. This was an experience I will never forget. My sorority positively impacted and shaped my life by bringing me lifelong friendships and opportunities to serve my community. There are so many memorable and indelible moments I had on the campus of Prairie View A&M University but walking across the stage to receive my degree and end my time on "The Hill" will always be a feeling that can't be erased. Prairie View gave me all the tools and time to go through a full *transformation*; now it was my time to *fly*.

Legacy (2017-Present)

Along with receiving two bachelor's degrees in biology and chemistry at Prairie View A&M University, Prairie View instilled so many characteristics in me that molded me into the person I am today. Sometimes, I look at my life and realize that many of my decisions were influenced by the wisdom that I gained at PV. At PV, I also found my lifetime partner, and am now engaged to my college sweetheart. I will forever be grateful for the HBCU experience. The culture and history of attending an HBCU are unexplainable. The friendships and lessons experienced enriched my life. College challenged and provided me with the necessary tools for success. I realized I could accomplish anything, which has pushed me to continue my education, become a serial entrepreneur, and a forever dreamer. Now as an educator in predominantly Black and brown communities, I am always advocating for the importance of education and the expression of creativity. I am an advocate of all higher learning but will always recommend an HBCU experience over anything, especially on "The Hill." When I speak on Prairie View University, it is always with *pride* and *joy*! I truly bleed purple and gold. Thank you, Prairie View A&M University.

About Kierra S. Jones

Kierra S. Jones is an educator with 5+ years of experience as a teacher and education consultant. She holds a Biology and Chemistry Degree from Prairie View A&M University and a Masters of Art in Urban Education with a concentration in Education Leadership.

Kierra partners with individuals, groups, and organizations to create highly engaging learning activities that support academic growth through her online platform Teaching Busy Bees LLC.

Kierra is also the founder and CEO of Booked Cafe Books, a children's diverse bookshop. Geared towards amplifying and empowering marginalized voices. Booked Cafe is "a bookshop rooted in giving back", for every book purchased another book is placed in the hands of a child or teachers hand free of charge.

Kierra currently lives in Dallas, TX, and uses her free time to explore the world through travel and adventure, self-care advocate, and spending time creating memories with her family and friends.

BERRIE RUSSELL

Producing Productive People
Berrie Russell

May 2014 was college night at my high school. I was so excited to go around and get information on the many colleges that were present. I stopped by at least three tables before I reached Prairie View A&M University's table. After reaching the PV table, I knew I was done searching. PV was the place for me. I applied to only one school and that was Prairie View A&M University—*my* HBCU! I knew choosing an HBCU would further the love I have for my culture and community, along with the opportunity to share that love with other like-minded young people.

While at Prairie View, I joined multiple organizations, but two stood out the most: Campus Activities Board and Delta Sigma Theta Sorority Incorporated. These organizations taught me patience, hard work, dedication, time management and most of all, *leadership skills*! Campus Activities Board is an organization that plans campus-wide events to maintain student engagement. I served as an executive board member on Campus Activities Board, and it was nothing short of a whirlwind! It was full of so many emotions, demanding work, time and dedication! So much school pride! There were eight of us on the executive board, and we were nothing short of a family!

During the time with the Campus Activities Board, I evolved every single year. I developed more, and I was developed more by one of my mentors and close friends, Orok Orok. At the time, he was the advisor for the Campus Activity Board. He helped me become who I already was with the traits I already had. This is something that you can only get at an HBCU—to have a Black leader, especially Orok Orok, to see something in you and develops you into another

Black leader! Then, you eventually develop other Black leaders! I got that experience firsthand, and I apply that to my life right now.

Campus Activities Board contributed so much to my growth— probably the most growth I've ever experienced in my life. I am so very thankful for my experiences. Campus Activities Board taught me how to be a better friend, a better leader, a better example and person overall. Campus Activities Board taught me that people are always watching, no matter what you do or say. It also taught me that everyone has different leading styles, and that's okay—take ownership of your individuality, and have confidence and pride in everything you do. As a member of Campus Activities Board, I was taught the difference between a good leader and a bad leader. I was taught the difference between black excellence and just being black. I was taught to be black excellence in every way by black excellence itself.

During my sophomore year, not only did I become an executive board member of the Campus Activities Board, but I also pledged to become a member of the illustrious Delta Sigma Theta Sorority, Incorporated. The Eta Beta Chapter of Delta Sigma Theta Sorority Incorporated was chartered December 19, 1969, by the Swinging 25. Being a member of Delta Sigma Theta, Inc. has changed my life tremendously. It has taught me the power of sisterhood, fellowship, networking and so much more. I've met so many women of so many backgrounds, but we all share one thing in common: we all are connected through *sisterhood*.

I remember the day I knew that I was going to be a Delta. During my freshman year, I attended a pajama event hosted by the Eta Beta Chapter. The event was for breast cancer awareness. No one knew at the time that my grandma passed due to breast cancer, so this topic was near and dear to my heart. This event wasn't your typical fun social event with sandwich cookies and cake; this event was amazing! This event was education and spiritual. Everyone wore their pink. We talked, we laughed, we prayed, we learned, and I wasn't even a Delta; I was just interested! It was an unforgettable moment, and I knew that day that I was going to be a Delta.

These ladies loved each other and loved other Black women. They desired to see other Black women to succeed in all ways. I loved it! Once I became a Delta, I still had that same feeling when my sisters and I hosted that breast cancer awareness event. I loved knowing and feeling the change I was making around my campus and my community, teaching, mentoring and growing with one another. Black women: the most powerful beings on this planet!

I love what we stand for! I love what we did on our campus and what we continue to do for our community today. I loved how we won sorority of the year two times in a row, how we set the bar and the example. How we were unstoppable! We were the ones to beat ever since we came on the yard, and we still are today! All of these experiences that I've learned while working in my organizations and studying biology, I had the courage and the drive to dive deep into entrepreneurship.

In summer 2017, I decided to start my business at Prairie View— The Perfect Glow TPGlow LLC. With the support and love of my friends, line sisters, mentors as well as staff, I was able to start my business. I started with making little hair concoctions out of my dorm room. I made a mixture of handmade hair creams and hair masks with all-natural ingredients like shea butter, avocado, bananas, yogurt, honey, and more. I would mix it, put it on my friends' hair and my line sisters' hair, and they loved it! I was encouraged to start my business, which was something I always wanted to pursue, but was just too afraid. I was caught up in fear and going through a mental battle I never knew I had. I started the business with body butters, BYOB (Build Your Own Butter) and I was doing well! Before I knew it, I reached a very dark time in my life, due to depression that brought me down!

I met with my dean about my mental health battle. She's such an amazing lady. She sat with me and allowed me to go home to get my mental health together. Instead of taking the entire semester off, I took an entire semester at home, still pursuing my education while working on my mental health. This is something that I feel you could also only get at Prairie View. She was very understanding and was willing to help me. The first thing that came to her mind was not only me finishing college successfully, but to have a sound mind and to be at peace. She made sure that I got the help I needed. While I was out of Prairie View A&M, she continued to check on me by email, text, and by phone to make sure I am good. To this day, we are still connected. I was blessed to have this experience at Prairie View A&M.

My dean exemplified what a true, loving, and compassionate leader is. As the dean, she is superior for my department, and she sets the tone. She showed me what the true meaning of leading with empathy was, and she gave me grace—something that I implement in my business and working life today. I took a hiatus with my business during that time, but that allowed me to time to heal and recover a sound mind. Now that I have graduated from Prairie View A&M University, I not only have a sound mind, but a successful day job and business.

Moral of this story: Prairie View is more than just college! It's an entire experience full of love, growth, and black excellence! The people you meet will become lifelong friends and family. The faculty you meet will become mentors and close friends. The pride you have for not only your university but for yourself will outgrow any pride you've had in your life. You will become a better you—a more self-loving, unapologetic, confident you!

I will end with this: *Prairie View Produces Productive People!*

About Berrie Russell

Berrie Russell the founder and CEO of The Perfect Glow was born in Dallas, Texas. She graduated from Prairie View A&M University in 2018. When she is not working fulltime on The Perfect Glow she is working in management for one of the largest companies in the world. In her free time she studies African American history as well as deep diving into selflove and selfcare living.

ALEXUS HALL

My Journey was Prolonged, but Worth the Ride
Alexus Hall

Prairie View A&M University produces productive people, and I am glad to say that I am one of them. I owe everything to "The Hill" because it helped me find myself and to begin my career in cybersecurity. My journey to graduation took me longer than I originally expected, but as I look back those extra years I spent at PV, they were worth it. There was beauty throughout the low moments I experienced. However, those moments guided me and taught me lessons that shaped me into the proud alum that I am today.

HBCUs have always been present in my life. Some of my family members attended HBCUs such as Southern University, Grambling University, Johnson C. Smith University, South Carolina State University, Dillard University, Prairie View A&M University, and Allen University. Growing up in a military family, no matter where we were stationed, my mother always found time to take us to the nearest HBCU football games and watch the band's halftime show. Every year, we visited family in New Orleans for Thanksgiving and watched the Bayou Classic on TV. Many times, we went to the Superdome to watch the game live or just browsed the streets and watched everyone repping their schools.

Since childhood, I've known about HBCUs and their impact upon our culture. Before I learned about PV, my plans were to major in computer engineering at institutions in Louisiana. My cousin, Erica Lewis (Class of 2008), told me about Prairie View, and I decided to add it to my list of schools to look at. When I went to Prairie View's website, they were one of the schools that offered my intended major. My mother and I decided to travel to PV and go to PantherLand Day, an event hosted on campus for prospective students. As soon as I stepped on campus, I had a feeling that this was where I wanted to be. The beauty of the campus, along with so many people rocking the purple and gold added to my excitement of being there. From touring the campus and the engineering building, to watching the band and the Greeks, I knew this was the school for me.

The College of Engineering implemented a new summer bridge program for incoming freshmen majoring in engineering called the "College of Engineering Enhancement Institute (CE2I)" in the summer of 2009. This program was developed to give incoming freshmen a glimpse of college life, along with all they can expect being an engineering major. We were privileged to meet many of the faculty members from the College of Engineering and from other parts of the university. Also, we took field trips and lived in the university college. At the time, one of the things I loved about the program was the advantage of getting ahead in some classes and already being moved into my dorm before the other incoming freshmen moved in. Coming from out of state, this program granted me a network of people before the fall semester even started and friends that I still stay connected with today.

Fall 2009 was the start of my freshman year. I was determined to hit the ground running, starting my collegiate career strong with the goals to be active and maintain a great GPA. The first semester, I did just that. I finished the semester with a 3.3 GPA, and I joined two organizations: Students in Free Enterprise (SIFE) and Toastmaster's International to stay active outside of school work. Joining these organizations taught me how to conduct business and introduced me to the foundational skills of free enterprise.

Every semester, the Career Service Department is over the Career Fair. During my first years at PV, I volunteered with setting up the booths and helping students get checked in. Whenever I had time, I would browse to see what companies would come and make sure I had resumes on hand. I learned just how competitive the job market was during these experiences. I can't even count how many times

I've gone to the career fair and felt like I didn't succeed. Of course, I had the organizational experience since I was active in that field; but after my first semester, my GPA kept fluctuating.

Being an engineering major was challenging. Some classes were easy, but the majority of the classes and coursework were difficult. Honestly, I don't think I would have made it through those classes without the homies who were "with me shooting in the gym." So many times, I would take notes in class and be lost; however, even though we struggled in classes sometimes, we tried to uplift and teach each other so that we could pass our classes. That's what I loved most about the COE family. Every class we took was a group effort because at the end of the day, we all were trying to graduate.

My last year at PV was the most challenging because of my senior design project. I was the team lead and overall responsibility for making sure the project was successful. The team's project was building an autonomous underwater vehicle (AUV). The project was also a part of a competition that was held during the summer in San Diego. In the competition, our AUV had to complete certain tasks to reach the next round of the competition. Our team reached the semi-final round in the competition, which was the furthest any team had gone previously since the College of Engineering started this project a few years ago.

Throughout my time at PV, I joined many organizations. For the first few years, I was heavily active in Students in Free Enterprise (SIFE) and Toastmaster's International, ultimately being elected as president of both organizations. I was tapped and inducted into Brothers Leading and Cultivating Knowledge (B.L.A.C.K.) and initiated into the greatest chapter of Kappa Alpha Psi Fraternity, Zeta Beta aka "The Zoo." These organizations helped me understand the importance of brotherhood and understanding politics at both university and country levels. Growing up, I wanted brothers and once I joined Kappa, I gained nineteen of them. Of course, we threw the best parties on the yard, but we also hosted amazing seminars and events on campus that benefitted all PV students. Traveling to other campuses and attending conferences not only showed me how great our chapter and university were, but how much of an impact we had on surrounding campuses.

One of the most fulfilling times I had at PV was my opportunity to work for Dr. Josette Bradford with the Panther Pride Summer Bridge Program as a counselor and later as an intern. Panther Pride was another program for incoming freshmen to get a piece of the college experience before the upcoming school year. This role was truly fulfilling because I was able to be a guide and mentor to the next class coming to PV. Through that program, we were able to start a mentoring initiative for the incoming male students called M.A.L.E., which stands for Men Achieving Leadership and Excellence with Dr. James Wilson, Dr. Michael McFrazier, Dr. Terence Finley, and Dr. Lucian Yates III. This initiative showed young men how to properly dress for business and provided mentorship on how to matriculate through college life. Essentially, M.A.L.E. equipped young men with the tools necessary for success once they leave Prairie View. From the initiative, I was able to be one of the students to represent PVAMU at the American Education Research Association (AERA) conference in Chicago, Illinois. At the conference, a group of us did a presentation entitled, "Images of Ideal Mentors: Perspectives of African American Male Students in the Men Achieving Leadership Excellence (M.A.L.E) Program." Through Panther Pride, I was fortunate to meet my brother and business partner David Hughes (Class of 2014). Together, we created an app called "Give Black" that allows Black businesses and organizations the place to receive funding directly from their donors.

Attending Prairie View A&M University was one of the best decisions of my life. This institution, along with the organizations I've participated in helped me become the man I am today. The leadership roles I obtained, the places I traveled, the mentors who guided me along the way, the friends and brothers who helped me through my good and the bad times, finding the love of my life, and my current career in cybersecurity can all be credited to being a PV student. Only God knows where I would be if I didn't attend Prairie View.

My journey at Prairie View took a little longer than I had expected. If I could do it all again, I would change a few things; but I still would choose "The Hill" every time. Anybody who knows me or has met me knows that I will always support and rock that purple and gold. Prairie View A&M was the best decision I made in my life, and I wouldn't know where I'd be if I decided to go elsewhere. I want to thank the many friends, family, mentors, and faculty that have guided me and continued to uplift me throughout my journey. Your advice and guidance gave me the push I needed to cross the graduation stage.

About Alexus Hall

Alexus is an Army kid and calls Louisiana home. Alexus is an Alumnus of Prairie View A&M University with a bachelor's degree in Computer Engineering (Class of 2016) and University of Dallas (Class of 2020) with a Masters degree in Information and Technology Management. He is the Co-founder & Chief Operating Officer, Give Black App. He is married to his amazing wife Brittany and has a dog named Rumi. Alexus currently resides in the DFW area working in Cybersecurity with Crowdstrike.

JACOLAHN DUDLEY

For Mem'ries Dear,

Jacolahn Dudley

I am forever indebted to Prairie View A&M University for the significant way it changed my life. Like many first-generation college students, I had very little knowledge about colleges, especially Historically Black Colleges and Universities. Truthfully, when I was first applying to college, I didn't even apply to Prairie View A&M University. It wasn't until my high school took seniors on a college tour and we visited Prairie View that I finally discovered this illustrious university.

During our campus tour, the students were so proud to tell us that they went to Prairie View. The faculty and staff around campus kept reminding us not to step on the grass, in addition to the story behind that sacred tradition. I recall the immense sense of pride everyone had for Prairie View. Throughout the day, we met and listened to students, faculty, staff and administrators who were all equally proud to tell the story of PVAMU and its impact upon students around the world.

My fondest memory about that day was the familiar campus atmosphere. Despite being just high school students, everyone at the institution made us feel like we were family and like PVAMU was our home. By the end of the day, I was in love with PVAMU. I made up my mind that I would be attending PVAMU after graduation. In fact, once I returned home that day, I told my entire family that I was going to PVAMU. I often tell people that I didn't choose Prairie View; Prairie View chose me. The day I stepped foot off that school bus in 2012, it was as if the university selected me to be a part of the family. For that, I am forever grateful.

While at Prairie View, I found myself, achieved unparalleled success, met lifelong friends, and was educated by some of the most brilliant minds in academia. Over the years, Prairie View allowed me to be challenged academically, to travel the world, and have several once-in-a-lifetime opportunities. Often times, people think of HBCUs as "lesser than institutions," but Prairie View is in the same category as other institutions. There were so many enormous opportunities that I was fortunate enough to be a part of because I attended Prairie View. Truthfully, many things that I accomplished and experienced would likely not have happened if I had attended a different institution. From traveling all over the country to attending the opening of the National African American Museum of History and Culture, representing Prairie View in television commercials and even speaking locally and nationally about the significance of PVAMU, the blessings I received as a PVAMU student were endless.

One of my most memorable experiences at PVAMU was my time as student body president. I went to college knowing that I wanted to get involved on campus. As I familiarized myself with the institution, it seemed that everyone at Prairie View who was involved and considered to be a student leader was a member of the Student Government Association. These students were leaders in many areas on campus and were all making a difference for the institution. I was so inspired by their initiatives that I knew I wanted to be a part of that change. Specifically, seeing students like Harrison Blair, Priscilla Barbour, and Jarrick Brown dedicated to serving the institution made me want to be a part of something greater than myself.

Eventually, I joined Student Government Association and served in various roles at all levels of the organization with hopes of one day becoming president. Fortunately enough for me, my dream became a reality—not once, but twice. As student body president, I was able to represent the thousands of students of Prairie View and work tirelessly to make positive changes for the betterment of the institution and its students, both current and future Panthers. Throughout my tenure, I implemented a suit scholarship for first-year students, organized a student recruiting ambassador program, signed the contract to bring the transportation service Zipcar to PVAMU, and a host of other accomplishments with the help of members of the Student Government Association. As someone who considers himself a difference-maker, my goal was to always leave the organization and the institution better than I had found it.

While at PVAMU, I was also able to develop some of the most impactful relationships that one could ever ask for. PVAMU was where I met my lifelong friends who have turned into family. I am so fortunate and blessed to have the same friends today that I first made five years ago. During my first year of college, the friends that I made helped shape my undergraduate experience. These friendships have been filled with laughter, crying, joy, pain, baby showers, weddings, birthdays, and graduations. I am also thankful to Prairie View for gifting me with the gift of brotherhood. Growing up as an only child, I am so thankful for Alpha Phi Alpha Fraternity, Inc., especially the brotherhood through the Eta Gamma Chapter. More specifically, to my line brothers of D.O.K., I am tremendously blessed to call you brothers in Alpha. These relationships have turned into lifetime relationships that I will cherish forever.

Since receiving my two degrees from PVAMU, I have accomplished monumental things throughout my professional career. The institution taught me how to be successful early on. While I may not have seen it at the time, Prairie View also equipped me with so many life lessons that I would eventually need in my personal and professional lives. I owe so much to Prairie View and to its faculty and staff members, who all significantly impacted my life. Because of my lessons learned while at Prairie View, this small-town boy from Beaumont, Texas, a first-generation college student, is a Ph.D. candidate at one of the top institutions in Texas.

I am so grateful for the men and women at Prairie View A&M University who saw so much potential in me that they decided to mold and nurture me into the epitome of what a Prairie View man should be. Individuals such as Mr. Steve Ransom, Dr. Michael McFrazier,

Dr. Josette Bradford, Mona Brown, Dean Lewter, Valerie Gibson, Melanie Porter, David Hughes, Dr. Mike, Dr. Nathan Mitchell, and the late Dr. James A. Wilson, Jr., poured so much into me throughout my time at Prairie View. I thank you all for mentoring me, listening to me, educating me, advocating on my behalf, encouraging me to be better, and most importantly, for never giving up on me. I can never truly thank you enough for your impact on my life.

As I close, I can't help but think about the words of O. Anderson Fuller in the last stanza of the Alma Mater; "we'll love thee now and through eternity." Out of all the lines in the Alma Mater, these words have always meant the most to me. Having a love for your institution makes your college experience much more memorable. Nevertheless, it is not just about loving your college or university during your tenure but loving that institution long after graduation. This love means joining an alumni chapter, being a financial contributor to your institution, whether large or small. This love also means volunteering at your institution when you have the time. This love means helping students get an internship, scholarship, or even a job offer. Ultimately, this love means that no matter what, you will always answer the call for Mother Prairie View when she needs you, because we pledged that we would love Prairie View, now and forever.

To Prairie View A&M University, I leave you with this. I love you and I thank you. I can never truly repay you for everything you have given me over the years. I am thankful for the relationships made, for the memories, experiences, and lessons learned. I am grateful for the way Prairie View developed me into the person I am today. My only hope is to give back just a fraction of what this institution has given me. If I can, I would be able to say that I have served my alma mater well.

About Jacolahn Dudley

Jacolahn is a proud native Texan born and raised in Beaumont, Texas. After graduating high school, Jacolahn attended Prairie View A&M University, receiving his B.A. in Political Science in 2017. While at PVAMU, Jacolahn was highly involved on campus and in the community and even served two terms as president of the Student Government Association. After receiving his undergraduate degree, Jacolahn went on to earn a Master's degree in Education Administration, also from PVAMU. Jacolahn works in student affairs at Georgetown University in Washington, D.C., and is also a Ph.D. candidate at the University of Texas at Arlington in the Educational Leadership and Policy Studies department. Jacolahn is a true servant leader passionate about student success, diversity, equity, and inclusion, and civic engagement. Jacolahn is also a proud member of Alpha Phi Alpha Fraternity, Inc.

JAMES DURANT

A Done Deal
James Durant

Dear Prairie View, our song to thee we raise.
In gratitude, we sing our hymn of praise.

These very words have always rung true in my life. To Prairie View A & M University, I owe my entire adulthood. Since childhood, I was told that I would have to attend a Historically Black College or University. Prairie View A & M University is my family's institution, having educated my great uncle, my parents, my aunts, my uncles, my cousins, and my sister. It was a no brainer that I would apply to PV and get accepted.

Growing up in Houston, Texas, Prairie View was like a second home for me. My parents took me to every homecoming, basketball game, and football game. So, PV is where I wanted to be. Entering college can be scary for anyone, and I was terrified. My mom had former students there and my dad was a charter member of the Alpha Phi Alpha Fraternity there. Plus, no one from my high school was attending PV.

I moved into my dorm and quickly made a friend in my roommate. Who knew that pairing the shy but loquacious student with an outgoing, ambitious student would change my life forever. After struggling in high school to make decent grades, I decided I was going to be a bookworm and not participate in any extracurricular activities. However, my roommate had other plans. He was a member of the Marching Storm Band and spoke to everyone. We always had people in the room playing on the PlayStation and talking about everything from music to the game to politics. My roommate noticed that I didn't do anything but study, so he encouraged me to get active on campus. Once he got me interested in activities, I couldn't stop!

And who would've thought I would become one of PV's top student leaders? My roommate came home from band practice one day and told me that the band was recruiting new members to go with them to Atlanta. Just like that, I got my saxophone, and my life began to play out to a new tune.

The Prairie View A&M University Marching Storm is the best band in the land! I was fortunate enough to join the band in 2004 with the largest crab class the Marching Storm had ever seen. Most of the friends I have to this day crabbed in the band with me. When I joined the band, I had already completed my freshman year at PV. So, crabbing my sophomore year made my experiences unique. By then, I was an active member in the Student Government Association, and I sat on a couple of university committees. However, my sister had just started her freshman year at PVAMU, and I did not want her to have the same issues that I had the previous year. So, I enrolled her in band with me. The marching band at any HBCU is always a unique experience. Often times, we are the superstars of the campus, but students really don't understand how much work, time, and effort goes into a rehearsal.

Juggling academics, student activities, and marching in the band became a struggle. The beginning of my sophomore year was not great. PVAMU's 2004 football schedule was difficult for the band. Within the first four games were Texas Southern University, Southern University, and the State Fair Classic with Gramling State. This meant *perfection* during the first game. Our largest three games were back-to-back-to-back. And if I learned nothing else from being in the Marching Storm, it was that every time we stepped toe to turf, we were to deliver the best pageantry anyone had seen. We were the *Entertainment Tonight!*

The major takeaway I got from the band had to come from the dynamic band director, Professor George W. Edwards. He always demanded perfection, talent, and your best work, which forced me to not only succeed as a band member, but it pushed me to do better academically as well. When you first meet Professor Edwards, you can feel intimidated. But after you get to know him, you would understand that he wants his students to graduate, grow, and be as successful as they can be. Professor believed that he could teach this lesson by having those same expectations in our practices and performances. Even when we got a standing ovation at a game, he would never say we did well because he always believed that we could do better.

That is one of the biggest lessons that I pass on to my students as a higher education professional. This is how I carry myself at work daily. I aspire to be as great to my students as George W. Edwards was to me. He was one of the first people at PV who realized my potential and put me in a leadership role that allowed me to represent the program to our university administration. I was probably one of the only students who was able to keep an entire program running without having an administrative assistant or business manager. My mission as a student worker was to take care of all the business of the band. This responsibility enabled me to learn the inner workings of higher education and become a determined student leader who got in every door that the campus ever had.

I have always joined clubs and organizations, but Prairie View A&M University's Student Government Association was a monster that I wanted to conquer. One of the biggest lessons that I've learned is you don't have to have the title of "president" to make decisions and influence people. You simply must know the rules and how things operate. I never became SGA president, even though that was one of my goals. However, I did have the opportunity to sit on multiple university committees just as an SGA senator because of my work ethic and flat-out ability to annoy administration by always being one of the most vocal students in the room.

Through SGA, I was able to meet Miss Betty Hall. Betty Hall attended PV with my parents, and she decided all my energy could be put to good use. Hired in as a student activities coordinator, Betty

Hall allowed me to shadow her as a student and taught me everything she knew about student activities. She was definitely the PV mother who would check me when I was wrong but dropped helpful hints on how to push the administration when I was right. She made sure that staff saw my potential and made me her go-to student. Because of her, I became so familiar with the university that it made me a shoo-in when I applied to be an orientation leader over the summer and a community assistant in University College. Those summers were some of the best years ever, and it set me up for my next journey.

University College is the first of its kind at an HBCU. This living and learning community was purposely developed to retain freshman and give them a "guided hand" into their university journey. As a community assistant, or in older terms, an RA, it was my responsibility to guide freshman at PVAMU. Along this path, I came across the legend, Ms. Yvette Barker. She was a "call-it-like-she-sees-it" housing director who did not play. She was always looking for the next student leader to come in and really push University College to be ahead of the times.

In University College, the community assistants were responsible for monthly programming. I always excelled at developing unique programming that had the entire property jumping. I worked in University College during my last two years at PVAMU. When I graduated, Ms. Barker offered me a job at PV as a learning community manager, i.e., a dorm director. This caused the spark that lit the fire that burns today. I would become a higher education professional for the rest of my life. From this job at University College, I began working at multiple HBCUs, changing the lives of numerous students and giving them a piece of the journey that I had at Prairie View A&M University.

There are so many brother and sister Panthers who have changed my life. My line brothers of Phi Mu Alpha Sinfonía Fraternity, Incorporated gave me brotherhood. My brother, Larry Allen, taught me how to lead the people by being yourself and being relatable.

Lastly, my family. Prairie View A & M University educated my parents, aunts, uncles, cousin, and my sister. My sister experienced this entire journey with me. She walked across the stage with me and helped me to get my degree. My parents were always proud of their journey at Prairie View, and I could not be any happier that they paved the way for me to experience the happiness and joy that shaped them to be the great people they are.

About James Durant

James L. Durant is a 3rd Ward Houston, Texas native. James is a 2008 graduate of Prairie View A&M University where he received his degree in Political Science with a minor in English. While attending Prairie View A&M University James was a member of the Marching Storm band program, Student Government Association, Campus Activity Board, University Newspaper, University Cheerleading program, a Community Assistant, and the Texas A&M's system student advisory committee. James is a Spring 2008 initiate and Member of Phi Mu Alpha Music Fraternity of America and a Fall 2018 initiate of Natchez Alumni Chapter of Kappa Alpha Psi Fraternity, Inc. An avid HBCU supporter, James has worked at multiple historically black colleges and universities and prides himself on developing the next generation of leaders of color. Currently, he serves as the Coordinator for Student Organizations and Greek Life at Texas Southern University. In 2021 he received his Masters in Workforce Education Leadership at Alcorn State University. He has a passion for programming and is a certified event and wedding planner. James' favorite quote is "Success is to be measured not so much by the position that one has reached in life as by the obstacles which he has overcome while trying to succeed."— Booker T. Washington

KHANAY TURNER, ESQ.

The Top Notch Legacy
Khanay Turner, Esq.

Many have heard the phrase, "My Parents raised me, but PV made me." The accuracy of that statement is sky true blue. When I stepped on the campus of Prairie View A&M University ("PV"), I felt the magical purple and gold flowing through my blood, passed down from my mother and from her parents, who are all alumni of this great institution. PV has continued to produce productive people throughout their 145 years of existence, and many are within this book. Nevertheless, this is my story and how I left my legacy on the greatest institution of higher education in Texas.

August 2011, I began a new chapter of my life at the second oldest public institution in Texas, Prairie View A&M University. At this historical university is where I found my calling to inform and educate my community about voter disenfranchisement. PV students have always held the torch to secure voting rights for college students, including giving them the right to vote in their college town. Even with this victory, PV students were still fighting to secure and protect their rights, even during my matriculation when the Texas Voter ID law first went into place and lack of a polling location on campus. I sought to bring more political awareness and involvement to my peers and the university administration.

I always knew that I wanted to be a public servant and help the Black community to attain true equality and equity, so being active on campus was nothing new. During my first semester of college, I became the only freshman to chair a Student Government Association ("SGA") committee, serving as the chairperson of the Political Action Committee. I promoted voter education and conducted a march to the polls for a local election. In addition, I established the PVAMU College Democrats, where I identified and recruited individuals who cared for the general welfare of our community and shared my passion for getting others involved in the 2012 election.

This passion for social justice led me to join other organizations that fought for these Causes. The biggest and dearest one to my heart is the Eta Beta Chapter of Delta Sigma Theta Sorority, Incorporated. I decided to take that leap of faith to pledge the greatest sisterhood in the universe that exuberates in fighting for social justice and political involvement. Not only was I a legacy, but Delta was synonymous with who I am and my purpose. Becoming a member of Delta Sigma Theta Sorority, Inc. opened many doors for me and allowed me to continue the work I started in SGA and with College Democrats.

In fall 2012, I hit the ground running to get students activated for the 2012 Presidential Election. I led my organizations in helping students get registered and update their documentation to prevent students from losing their right to vote over minor technicalities. Students were educated on the acceptable IDs, informed of who was on the ballot, and the Candidate's campaign issues from the U.S. President to the county judge. As Social Action Chair for Eta Beta, I organized several candidate forums, debate watch parties, and marches to the polls. One of my biggest successes was organizing the 2012 election watch party, where over one thousand people from the university and surrounding community came together to watch and experience the reelection of President Barack Obama. This was the largest event held by a student organization outside of SGA to that date. The most important part is that students became engaged in the political process and wanted to do more for their community.

In the summer of 2013, I interned in the office of U. S. Congresswoman Marcia Fudge and I was elected as the Collegiate Member of the National Nominating Committee of my illustrious sorority during our Centennial National Conference. I became Eta Beta's first nationally elected board member, which ignited other members of the chapter to run and be elected as members of the national board for the next three years. To be elected during Delta's Centennial, while serving as a congressional intern for a past National President was something I would never imagine. I had the support from my professors, sorors and administration to ensure that I did not fail. That summer taught me a lot about the power of PV and our network. I was honored to have represented my institution with excellence.

Junior year, I stepped up into the role of a senator in SGA and became a community assistance (CA) with the university student housing, expanding my reach with more students to understand their needs. Throughout the year, I continued to expand voter education to my peers and held community forums to make them aware of the issues impacting them outside of election season. Prairie View A&M University is the largest employer in Waller County and the students are a major voting bloc; therefore, it was imperative that the students also knew what actions were being taken on their behalf in the community. We were more than the group of "Black kids making noise or trouble." We had the power to make real change in Waller County, and the elected officials needed to know that we refused to be oppressed.

As my final year began, I was established as the liaison between the community and the students when it came to politics in Waller County. The biggest candidate event I facilitated was hosting a rally for 2014 Democratic Texas gubernatorial candidate, Wendy Davis. This was the first time a Texas gubernatorial candidate had held a rally at PV, placing the university on the map as a campus for major statewide candidates to visit in years to come. This opportunity allowed candidates to learn about this great institution and the contributions PV students have brought to the nation.

The growing involvement of PVAMU College Democrats within politics gave me the chance to serve on the national board of the College Democrats of America as the National Director of African

American Affairs. As a board member, I had the opportunity to attend the 2015 Democratic National Committee Winter Conference, where President Obama was the keynote speaker. Not only was I able to be present for this intimate moment, but I was selected to sit in the front row and shake President Obama's hand. None of this could have been possible without the financial support of PV's administration and our incredible advisors who continue to advocate for College Democrats' presence in rooms of opportunity.

In my final semester, I wanted to ensure that the Class of 2015 had a special commencement with a special speaker. For the past three and a half years, PV's President, Dr. George C. Wright had served as commencement speaker. It was time for a change, so I started a survey with a list of potential speakers for the May 2015 Commencement which included Tom Joyner, Nikki Giovanni, Lance Gross, PV's own Congressman Emmanual Cleaver, and Dr. George Wright. In three days, 240 seniors responded with a majority for Tom Joyner to speak. I set up a meeting with the administration to discuss the students' request to have a new commencement speaker. During that meeting, the administration seemed surprised that the students had requested a guest speaker but understood the students' desires. Unfortunately, I was told that they didn't have the "funding" for a guest speaker for commencement. This was a total disappointment; however, a respectable relationship with Dr. Wright was established, which allowed me to come to him directly for future concerns. By fall 2015, the decision to have a guest commencement speaker was made, and for the December 2015 Commencement, Major General Julius Parker, Jr. delivered the commencement address. I could not have been prouder of the simple yet significant change of the impact I had made on my university.

Prairie View made me the woman I am today. It gave me a space and platform to discover who I am in this world. It provided me with an incredible support system, from my closest friends and sisters to the most incredible professors who continued to believe in me even when I did not. Not only did I excel with leadership on campus and in the community, but I also excelled in my academics, graduating summa cum laude. Over the years, I have continued to reach back anytime my professors call on me to engage their students in the political process. I will forever hold and represent Prairie View A&M University throughout my life.

About Khanay Turner, Esq.

Attorney Khanay Turner is the managing attorney and owner of the K.Y. Turner Law Firm, PLLC. She is a native of Fort Worth, Texas, and a proud graduate of two HBCUs, Prairie View A&M University and Thurgood Marshall School of Law at Texas Southern University.

Attorney Khanay has always been an activist and a social engineer since her time at Prairie View A&M University and throughout law school. Prior to launching the K.Y. Turner Law Firm, Attorney Khanay had an extensive career within government and public affairs. She has served as Chief of Staff for Texas State Representative Toni Rose, Executive Director for the Texas Legislative Black Caucus, and the Political Outreach Director for the Beto O'Rourke Senatorial Campaign. Attorney Khanay is still heavily involved with community grassroots outreach, as she serves as the Director of Operations and Programs for the Barbara Jordan Leadership Institute.

During both undergraduate and law school, Attorney Khanay has interned for Congresswoman Marcia Fudge, Congressman Marc Veasey's campaign, National Parks Service, Wendy Davis' gubernatorial campaign, Earl Carl Institute for Legal and Social Justice, and the U.S. Attorney Office of the Southern District of Texas. Attorney Khanay aspires to be the voice for the voiceless of all disenfranchised people.

Attorney Khanay is an active member of the following organizations:

- Fort Worth Alumnae Chapter of Delta Sigma Theta Sorority, Inc.

- NAACP Tarrant County Branch and NextGen

- DFW Urban League Young Professionals

- BRIDGE Young Professional

- L Clifford Davis Legal Association.

KIANDRA DANIELS

You're Never Really Alone
Kiandra Daniels

"Come on y'all, we gone miss the band," my mama said to my family. With my hand in hers and the other clutching a Fletcher's corndog, we weaved through the crowd at the State Fair, aiming for the Cotton Bowl. Every year for as long as I can remember, my mama made it a point to pack up me, my older brother, and other family members who wanted to come, and head to Dallas for what I'd argue to be the most iconic football game in Texas: *The State Fair Classic*. I was never disappointed by this experience. To see so many people who looked like me celebrating themselves, cheering on their favorite HBCU, and dancing along to the cadence of the bands were inspiring to me even at my early age.

The State Fair Classic is a rivalry football game between Grambling State University and the prestigious, illustrious Prairie View A&M University. I think I've only missed one year my entire life. Before I got to the point in my childhood where I could make my own decisions, my mama had us sitting on Grambling's side every year. I never asked why she was such a fan, but I forgive her. Anyway, as I got older, there was something alluring about PV. I'm not sure if it was noticing the pride of their students and fans in the stands, or if it was falling in love with The Marching Storm. Whatever it was, by the time I was a senior in high school, I knew that I wanted to go to Prairie View.

Of course, I was encouraged to apply to other schools (PWIs), and I was accepted by all of them with academic scholarship offers. Prairie View was the only school to offer me a four-year scholarship. Some may think, "Oh well she only went for the money." I admit that the scholarship was a definite plus that sealed the deal; however, growing up in a small town where people had limited options to leave, this was a huge opportunity for me that I could not afford to refuse. On top of that, I was also around people who looked like me. I had the experience of being taught by Black teachers and coaches. They were always warm and went the extra mile. I honestly believe that if it weren't for them, I would have ended up in a different place. They helped build my confidence to a place that propelled me to where I am today. I wanted to continue receiving that level of comfort. I wanted to go to a university where I would feel at home. Prairie View was that place for me.

As exciting as it was to make this decision, I think most of us probably experienced a sense of grief when we actually made the move. I struggled with feeling homesick for much of the beginning of my first year. Unfortunately, I missed the experience of moving in during Panther Week. After my mama and aunt got me all moved into my dorm in the UC the following weekend, I thought, "What now?" As I put my things away and tried to make my space feel like home, I felt some anxiety creep in. I thought of leaving my friends and family behind. I thought of having to start over from graduating from high school with a high status, to learning how to make new friends and find myself all over again. I had a couple of cousins and one good friend who was already there, but I still had one foot lingering in my old relationships and life. I did not know how to let go of high school life.

My norm is to be observant and quiet in a room full of people I do not know. I still have to fight my shyness at times, even to this day. It wasn't until I started to go out to some campus events that I started to feel that familiar safety I hoped for. My first big event that impacted me was going to probate. At that time, I was not too familiar with Greek life, so I was very astonished by all the organizations, particularly Zeta Phi Beta Sorority, Inc. It was awfully close to what I felt the first time I watched the Marching Storm all those years ago—*awestruck*. I was already slowly getting used to campus life, but that day stirred a desire within me to make more connections and network outside and inside of the classroom. I decided that I needed to come out of my shell and start showing people around me that I wanted to be more than just a student.

When I was in high school, I was incredibly involved and well known in my community. It dawned on me after watching probate that that involvement was what was missing. Being out and truly on my own, I had to learn to expand my anxiety window by doing things I normally did not have to do in the past. I needed to talk to people who could become a part of my journey.

I started talking to my CAs and to my freshman advisor. I tried to make connections with at least one professor each semester, and I made more friends and associates through the cousins and friend I had. Once that first year was over, it became easier and easier for me to continue to build these lasting relationships that helped me along the way.

During my sophomore year, I explored more events to feel out what direction I wanted to go in. At this time, I started to get into some of my core classes and meet psychology professors who gave me options on what career path to take. By my junior and senior years, I'd built lasting friendships, networked with professionals that put my name in places I previously would not have been, and I became a member of organizations such as Panther Advisor Leaders (PA…LS!) and The Smooth and Dominant Omega Gamma Chapter of Zeta Phi Beta Sorority, Inc. I had everything that I needed to graduate from PV with success. I was also able to leave a legacy that would inspire others who came from similar backgrounds as me to have dreams of attending an HBCU.

Although my initial post-graduation plan to work in mental health for a year before heading back to school did not work out, my connections led me back to PV for my first year of graduate school in the Marriage and Family Therapy program. That's when I really felt the strength and confidence in becoming a Black therapist who specializes in serving black mental health.

Today I am a licensed marriage and family therapist in Texas. I own a private practice, Color Wheel Therapy, PLLC, that focuses on improving black mental health by normalizing the need for services and conversations. I believe that I would not have been as affirmed, prepared, or as inspired to take on such a massive responsibility to my community if I did not attend Prairie View A&M University. I am a living testament that Prairie View truly does produce productive people.

About Kiandra Daniels

My name is Kiandra Daniels; I graduated from Prairie View A&M University in Spring 2014. I am currently a Licensed Marriage and Family Therapy Associate in Texas, and I run my own private practice, Color Wheel Therapy, PLLC. Born and raised in Tyler, TX, I was blessed with being surrounded by a family-oriented community. From the schools and neighborhoods, I always felt supported and encouraged. I decided to pursue my bachelor's degree in Psychology at PVAMU because I felt that it would be the perfect place to continue receiving that sense of family while gaining the necessary education to achieve future goals. While attending, I became a member of Zeta Phi Beta Sorority, Inc. and Panther Advisor Leaders where I was able to provide service to fellow panthers and local communities. Today, I am an accomplished therapist working to improve mental health in Black individuals and families.

SKIP WILSON

Iron Sharpens Iron
SKIP Wilson

In 2020, I was honored to be chosen as a contributing author for the book, *The HBCU Experience, The Band Alumni Edition*. I was very excited because I had an opportunity to be a published author. To my surprise, it was charted as an Amazon "fast mover." Then, it went on to be on the bestseller's list. I was beside myself with joy. I told the story of my freshman year at Prairie View A&M University, and I received plenty of great feedback. One of my friends actually said to me, "Okay cool, that was chapter one; now, where's the rest of your book?" I laughed and said "Soon, coming soon." Who would have imagined that I would be contacted again and asked to be a contributing author for the next book in the trilogy? I was honored and grateful, and that's why I'm calling this chapter, "My Chapter 2."

Prairie View A&M University is affectionately known as PV or as "The Hill." PV has a rich history of pride and excellence, and I was oblivious to all of it. Before I enrolled at Prairie View, the band was all that I knew about. By the end of my freshman year, I was one hundred percent a Panther. The people who I've met over the years and hung out with are still my friends to this very day. The atmosphere at PV not only made it a school of higher learning, but it also made it a home away from home.

All of my time was split between classes, the band, studying, and hanging out and partying There was almost never a dull moment. The professors that I had encountered made sure that you turned your assignments in on time because they cared about us passing and excelling. They gave us assignments that were due on Friday because they knew the students would do them early. The reason is because on Thursdays, almost no one did homework because most of the parties would be on Thursday nights. This was the case because most people went home on Friday afternoons. If there wasn't a football or basketball game, a step show or party on the weekend, PV was virtually a ghost town with the exception of a few people who didn't leave. So, you had to do your assignments by Thursday. We called it "Thirsty Thursday." It was just a thing that we did on the Hill. But every once in a while, a few professors would still have a mandatory test on Friday just to make sure that our priorities were in order.

As I'm sitting here reminiscing and typing, I can't help but to understand and realize all that Prairie View has done for me. In the grand scheme of it all, I was fortunate to have found my way to PV because my life could have been a whole lot different. I met several professors that not only expected a lot out of me, but they inspired me to be better than who I was. I had three band directors at PV who all saw my gift and allowed me to hone my skills—skills that actually took me further than I could ever imagine. Professor George Edwards (Rest in Peace), Dr. Mark Phillips, and Professor Larry Jones were three of these men, and I can't forget Dr. Margaret Sherrod, she was the founder of the world famous "BLACK FOXES," the majorette and dance line for the band. Dr. Sherrod always had words of encouragement.

Band was in my DNA—my Dynamic Natural Ability. I had a knack at it, and they allowed me to experiment with ideas for the band, as well as the drumline, which was better known as "The BOX." In 1989, Professor Edwards asked the two section leaders of the BOX, Joe Jackson and Rodney Goods, to create a show in a show. What that meant was at halftime, in the middle of the halftime show, he was going to carve out about two minutes for the drumline to do our own separate show—a show in a show. They wrote the first part of the show, which is now known as a Feature; but then, all of a sudden, it took on a life of its own. That's when the creativity of the other BOX members came in and it all gelled together. The first Feature was born.

Professor Larry Jones was the percussion instructor. He allowed us to experiment with a watchful eye, and he knew that we were stepping into unchartered waters. We didn't know it, but we had just created what is now known as, Show Style Drumming. The game that we were to showcase the newly devised show in a show, was for our second biggest rivalry, the Grambling State University Tigers. Although Texas Southern University is our number one biggest rivalry because they about an hour away, the Grambling game was our biggest game because it was the opening of the State Fair in Dallas. This event drew a crowd of about 65,000 people, so we were hyped. Needless to say, when the BOX performed the Feature, the crowd went crazy—not just Prairie View's fans, but the whole stadium erupted in cheers and a standing ovation. Yep, we were onto something, and Professor Edwards and Professor Jones were too proud of us.

Over the next few years, my college life was a see saw. I had stopped taking loans for school because I realized when I was a sophomore that I didn't want the debt that college loans would burden me with. I had a job, so I moved off campus and paid for my own school tuition. So, that meant going to school for a semester and being out for a semester. That was okay for me at the time because sometimes, I would be focused on school and other times I wouldn't. In 1994, I told Professor Edwards that I really didn't want to march anymore after that year, and he agreed that I needed a change. So, he offered me the job to be the assistant to Professor Jones for the 1995 school year, but the stipulation was that I focused on school, and I agreed. The BOX was, and still is, the most influential drumline in the HBCU world and beyond. My last year with Prairie View's drumline was in 2009 when Prof. Edwards died from complications resulting from a car accident. I miss my mentor every day, his fatherly advice, his fussing, his words of wisdom, and his guidance. He was a great man who inspired the masses. I see all of my teaching style in him.

Prairie View is one of those places that will bring the best out of you. Our motto is P.P.P.P., which means *Prairie View Produces Productive People*. I apply this motto to my life every day. In my professional life, I've been working for the largest moving and transportation company, United Van Lines, for thirty-seven years. This is the job I had when I entered Prairie View A&M University. I've since walked up the proverbial ladder in my industry and I'm doing well. At the same time that I had a regular job, I was teaching at-risk children how to play drums. Since 1998, I have been giving kids the skills they needed to get into major universities on band scholarships, inspiring kids to break the cycle of poverty, and mentoring young men and women to the idea that the cards that they were dealt, didn't have to be the cards that they had to play. I can honestly say that I helped hundreds—if not thousands of kids to go to college. I even created and founded the Prairie View Marching Storm Band Alumni association in 2003, geared towards promoting a positive band experience and scholarships.

Prairie View A&M University means a lot of things to a lot of people; but to me, it always brings a feeling of pride and honor to my soul and to my spirit. I met the mother of my beautiful daughter, Tameka Jhonye' Wilson, whom I affectionately call T.J., at Prairie View. I am also proud to have met Dr. Johanna Thomas Smith and Mrs. Edmunds in the English department, and Dr. Janice Beal and Dr. Peter Metofe in the Psychology department. These four people inspired my understanding and pushed me to be better. I have no idea where I would have been without Prairie View, but I know where I am because of Prairie View A&M. Let's just say that PV made me a better me and that was exceedingly more than I ever imagine to be. Prairie View Produces Productive People and I am a proud Panther for life. The greatest part of my journey was always knowing that I had the support of my family and friends and that is the greatest sense of security that any man can have.

About SKIP Wilson

I am a native Houstonian that fell in love with drums at an early age. It all started by me taking the pots and pans out of the cabinets and driving my mother crazy by constantly beating and beating while she was trying to cook. One day a friend of mine that lived five houses down from me, mother, threw away his Muppet's drum set. I saw it and I asked her if could I have it and she said yes. I was nine years old and this ironically was the start of a lifelong love of playing drums. Although that toy drum set didn't last but about two weeks, my love and passion flourished. The very next year, I was in the 6th grade and God gave me a band class and the band director, Mr. Hurdle let me choose the drums and I excelled. I later attended Kashmere Senior High School and the band director Mr. LeBlanc encouraged and demanded creativity so that's what we did, created. At Kashmere there were four brothers, the Taylor Boys Ricky, Pat, Mack, and Terry, that had all the style and pizazz that made for a pitri dish of creativity, style, love, and showmanship. We had a very good drumline. Then in 1987 I graduated and once again, God intervened, I enrolled at Prairie View A&M University and Majored in Psychology and Minored in English and this is where I met Professor George "Prof" Edwards and I "crabbed" (became a freshman member) In the greatest HBCU Band in the world. The drumline at Prairie View was called The PV McFunk BOX, "THE BOX" for short and they were the next level of playing and performing with a drum, I knew that I was home. I excelled, my drum skills and my creativity exploded and I helped create a style of drumming called "SHOWSTYLE". When my years of service to The BOX as far as performing was at its end, Prof. Edwards made me the the Assistant Percussion instructor assisting Professor Larry Jones with The BOX. This relationship lasted until May of 2009 when unfortunately Professor Edwards died from complications due to a car wreck. In

2003 I founded the Prairie View "Marching Storm" Band Alumni Association geared towards bridging the gap between the different eras of the band from the 1960's through the 2000's and raising much needed money that the band needed for equipment and scholarships. I've volunteered and taught at several at-risk High Schools in the Houston area and helped facilitate scholarships to multiple colleges and universities. Some of those schools are Madison High School 98-99, Thurgood Marshall High School 2002-2006, North Forest High School 2009-to present, Alto Senior High School 2015 to present and I also consult and teach at Forest Brook Middle School which is the feeder school to North Forest High School. This was journey and I will do it as long as God wants me to.

CALVIN FORD

The Hill
Calvin Ford

At some point in everyone's lives, there comes a crossroad where you must decide the next level of your life's journey. I encountered my first crossroad during my senior year in high school after I had decided to attend Prairie View A&M University. In the midst of trying to decide whether or not I was going to play football in college, I suffered a knee injury during a football game and really never fully recovered from it. College football was another level where the players were faster and bigger, so I knew that my injury would slow me down drastically. I decided to attend Prairie View and focus on the degree I would be pursuing.

The greatest character building and foundation of my life's journey formed while attending, in my personal opinion, the greatest HBCU in the country! Trust me; I know others beg to differ with that statement because they feel the same way about their HBCU, but that's what makes that connection so marvelously great because no matter what HBCU any of us attended, they all are great!

My wonderful experience at Prairie View started in the fall of 1984 immediately when my father and mother passed the entrance of the university. Seeing those flagpoles and a sign reading, "Welcome to Prairie View A&M University," I felt like I finally made it to my foundation and destiny in life. Lo and behold, I really could not have imagined the life's experiences, people and lifelong friends that were vastly awaiting me.

As we were checking into the world-famous Holly Hall freshmen dorm, I spotted one of my friends and high school classmates who had already checked into his room. He helped my father and me unload my things.

If you attended a HBCU, then some of you have said these words after your mother and father and/or whoever dropped you off and left the campus: "It's on Now!" By that first weekend after moving in the dorm, I ran into several of my friends from high school. I met several new ones as those first couple of weeks went by. At last, I am officially a Panther! I was extremely excited to be on campus and in the midst of all the other students, trying to register for classes and getting frustrated like many! After a few of my friends who were sophomores saw how hard of a time I was having trying to navigate through the chaotic process, they showed me the ropes and I finally got registered. I met several administrative staff members who would be very pivotal to my experiences as a student at Prairie View.

I never really met any strangers, so Prairie View afforded me the opportunity to meet so many people early in my first semester that some thought I was a sophomore rather than a freshman. I had friends who graduated from my high school and had joined a Non-Greek Coed Organization (Wisconsin Sleepers, Inc.). They encouraged me to come to the smoker and get some information about the organization. I, along with about eighty other students attended and again, I saw some old friends and made new ones that evening. Next thing I know, I was on line pledging and had no idea what I had gotten myself into! After nearly two months pledging, we finally went over and were the newest members of the Wisconsin Sleepers, Inc. This ended up being one the best decisions I ever made outside of deciding to attend Prairie View because it introduced me to the community service world that I operate in presently.

Life on campus was wonderful, being a member of a very popular organization and truly experiencing that real HBCU experience. I loved the fact that the university really supported student organizations and allowed us to express our pride in our organizations on campus. Just seeing each section with a tree that each organization had painted with their colors, shields, etc. was extremely exhilarating. The main gathering location on campus was another famous building named, "The Alumni Hall," which was the cafeteria where students would hang out after lunch and dinner. Some of the best moments were when all the fraternities, sororities and other organizations would have their pledgees out along with everyone just gathering and enjoying themselves. This was the heart of the campus. Many memories were made at Alumni, sitting around the fountain with everyone else whether you were a part of an organization or not.

After a few semesters of subpar grades from too many extracurricular activities, I experienced a devastating eye opener: academic probation, a couple of times! Of course, my parents were very upset and threatened to make me come home because I was not on a scholarship or grants. Here we go again; I approached another crossroads in my life. I had to decide if I was going to disappoint my mother and father and waste their hard-earned money to even give me the opportunity to further my education. Like any parent, they wanted us to make something of ourselves. So, I got focused and turned myself around. I did what I knew I should have done from the beginning—take care of my business in the classroom. I realized that I not only had to make my parents proud of me, but I had to do it for *myself*!

There's nothing like when "that light comes on" within you and illuminates your remembrance, reminding you that you have some of the most intelligent, caring, professional, and highly educated African American professors in place to help you reach your educational and professional goals. I buckled down, sat on the front row, concentrated and did my homework immediately after class. I was majoring in business management and was under the leadership of the Dean of the Business College at the time, who was Dr. Barbara Jones. Whether it was in high school or college, everyone had that one professor who did not play at all! Dr. Jones was that professor. For some reason, she stayed on me from the first time I took her class until I graduated. As stated earlier in my educational experience, I had a few subpar semesters, and Dr. Jones was one of the professors who failed me in her class and made me take her class again. After I had my "come to Jesus" moment with myself, I studied, and did not receive anything less than a 3.0 GPA the last two years of college.

It was time for graduation, and the seniors could not wait to get that one letter that said, "You have completed your degree curriculum and will be able to graduate with the next graduating class." I got my letter and to be honest, I was a little nervous. When I opened it, I saw that I did it—I was going to graduate. I hollered with excitement in the hallway during the passing of classes! Everyone who received theirs did the same. Dr. Jones was in the hallway and said something so profound to me that I will never forget it! Knowing all along that she already knew because she signed off on it, she said, "Mr. Ford, how did you get that letter of graduation confirmation?"

"I studied and passed all my classes, Dr. Jones!" I respectfully yelled.

"I knew all along that you had it in you, Mr. Ford," she said, smiling. "It was up to you to see your potential and you did it and I'm proud of you!" I will never forget that statement.

My experience at Prairie View A&M University was liberating. It opened up doors for me that I would have never been able to walk through had I never made those crossroad decisions. Receiving my B.B.A. in Business Management in 1990 from Prairie View has afforded me a career with the United States Department of Agriculture Food and Nutrition Service for thirty years. I would be remiss if I did not mention the memberships in several organizations that have built the frame of my vast experience with community service: The Wisconsin Sleepers, Inc., Prince Hall Affiliated Masons, DeSoto Panthers Youth Football & Cheerleading Organization, Omega Psi Phi Fraternity, Inc. and the Inspiring Body of Christ Church, which all have been the driving source in serving my community. No matter where I am, I'm thankful for my HBCU Experience at "The Hill."

About Calvin Ford

Calvin Ford was born December 13, 1965 in Dallas, Texas to the parents of the late Calvin Ford, Sr. and Luvenia J. Ford. He grew up in Oak Cliff and attended Birdie Alexander Elementary School and Hulcy Middle School. He then attended David W. Carter High School where he played Football and graduated in 1984. After graduating high school, Calvin attended Prairie View A&M University located in Prairie View, Texas in which he graduated and received his B.B.A. in Business Management in 1990. Calvin is married to Stephanie Ford and they have two children, Calvin III and Courtney.

Calvin community service/outreach began while attending Prairie View when he became a member of the Wisconsin Sleepers, Inc., a coed social service non-Greek organization. He found his passion serving the community there at Prairie View and was elected the organization's President from 1988 until he graduated. After graduating, Calvin continued to be very involved in the community and served as the Wisconsin Sleepers, Inc. National President from 1991-1993, 1999-2001. He also served as the Dallas Alumni Chapter President for several years and was a founding member of a newly established chapter at Paul Quinn College.

Calvin begin his government career with the United States Department of Agriculture (Farm Service Agency) in 1992 and later transferred to the United States Department of Agriculture (Food and Nutrition Service) in 1999. He is currently a Program Specialist monitoring the National School Lunch Program in the Southwest Region that consists of seven states (Texas, Oklahoma, Arkansas, New Mexico, Louisiana, Utah, and Arizona). Calvin is an accomplished leader with a proven efficiency to support United States Department of Agriculture (USDA) Food and Nutrition Service (FNS) strategic priorities with demonstrated knowledge and proficiency in interpreting and applying pertinent laws, regulation, policies, and procedures affecting FNS Programs.

Calvin joined the Desoto Panthers Youth Football & Cheerleading Organization as a coach in 1998 in the Dallas area. After a few years of coaching, his leadership skills was noted by the President of the organization at the time, and was asked to take over the organization as the new President in 2005 and is still serving as the President of the organization today.

Calvin is also a proud member of the Omega Psi Phi Fraternity, Inc. where he is actively serving in the Omicron Upsilon Chapter in Waco, Texas. He participates in serving the surrounding communities in Waco and the southwest areas of Dallas.

Calvin is a proud member of the Inspiring Body of Christ Church where Pastor Rickie G. Rush is the pastor. He serves as an Usher.

SIDNEY LEBEAUF

The Best Timing is Now
Sidney LeBeauf

The night of freshman move-in, it all hit me: I had just moved into a dorm room and for the next four years, I would be nearly 400 miles away from home — doing my best to figure out this next chapter of life on my own.

There was so much about college that I did not know about at that time. At the very start of my collegiate career, my sole mission was to stay focused, get my degree, make friends along the way and, of course, enjoy the pomp and circumstance of being a college student. What I did not realize is just how pivotal Prairie View would be towards my personal development—not only as a student, but as a professional, among other things.

During Freshman Orientation Week, I got acclimated to the feel for the campus and settled into Building 43 where I met other engineering majors. It was there that I started to develop a network of people who were likeminded, with a common goal of getting an engineering degree. I chose to study Civil and Environmental Engineering and knowing there were folks that I would see every day embarking on the same journey gave me confidence, along with wanting to see everyone find their way to their own personal successes. A few of us instantly connected so when classes began, we would study and do homework in tandem. If we had a group project, we would try to work together to continue fostering this sense of familiarity for the coursework and community amongst ourselves. Though I entered college with the thought of home being so distant, I gained comfort in knowing that I could go down the hall to talk if needed. If we were up late and hungry, we would find a way to get to Hempstead or Cypress to grab a bite to eat. We could work together, utilize our resources, and find a way to make our time away from home more comfortable while pursuing our higher education goals – all of this was meaningful.

Knowing that my future was paramount, I was eager to participate in the first career fair. My community assistants set up a résumé building workshop for Building 43 to ensure we had the correct information, our resumes were formatted properly and were presentable, and that we were prepared to attend the career fair as first-year students. The mere fact that our development—even as first-year students—was a priority, spoke volumes. I knew I could now go to the career fair prepared to present myself to the companies I had wanted to work with. I went and landed an interview with a big company, which undoubtedly boosted my confidence. This opportunity made me believe in myself tenfold, simply knowing this company saw value in me.

As time went on, I noticed that there was always a family aspect of things at Prairie View A&M University. There was always someone for me to use as a resource. Everybody at the university were there for one another. We were about each other and there to see the university continue to grow. And this quickly solidified that the idea of *community* was not a trend, but a constant theme. My camaraderie with my dorm mates was just the beginning.

The Community Assistants (CAs) on the Second and Third floors of Building 43 were a part of an organization called B.L.A.C.K.— Brothers Leading and Cultivating Knowledge. The group always seemed to be doing something to benefit the campus or community, with things like voter registration and cafeteria cleanups. That always stood out to me because I had never seen a group of young Black men pushing for civic engagement and pushing the culture in the right direction. Unbeknownst to me at the time, I would later become a part of that same organization. There was the SGA President, SGA Vice President, the President of the National Society of Black Engineers, and so many other brothers in leadership roles that I could not imagine myself in. Getting to know the members of the organization and the stories of the individuals within the organization led me to think about college, and life, in a unique way. I always wanted more for myself and the members of B.L.A.C.K. were moving towards the "better" for themselves. I would later join the Student Government Association, the American Society of Civil Engineers, National Society of Black Engineers, PALS, the African Student Association, to keep myself active. What I did not realize is that I would continue to make connections and develop relationships with people who I consider friends to this day.

Student Government Association was a pivotal part of my development. Through my positions as the Senator for the College of Engineering and the Vice President of Auxiliary Services, I had the opportunity to meet with the President of the University, the Associate Provost of Academic Affairs, the Dean of the College of Engineering, the Vice President of Business Affairs, the Vice President of Auxiliary Services, and many others. These connections and relationships allowed me to see the university not only from the student's perspective, but also from an administrator's perspective. The administrators were not just there to do a job and leave, my conversations also came with challenges from the administration to the student body, including myself. But these experiences were just a start for my journey within SGA.

During the Spring of 2014, I made the decision to run for President of Student Government Association. This campaign was the ultimate challenge for me, considering I'm more of a reserved person. The role would give me the opportunity to continue the things that I had been working on through the past couple years in SGA and I wanted to take on the challenge of being the person to take the baton on the next leg of the university's growth. Campaigning for President allowed me to get out of my comfort zone and to push myself to do something that I was enthusiastic about.

On election day I seemed to be the most at peace and regardless of the results I would have been satisfied with my effort to share my vision for the university. I won the election and for the next year, I made a concerted effort to deliver on the key components of my campaign and balance life as a full-time student. The entire year presented many challenges personally and academically. Being a leader is a special task and being an effective leader is an even greater endeavor. This was a time where, as much as I felt that I should be speaking up, I needed to be an attentive listening and hear the needs of all. Then the work became about sharing those voices with the people making decisions. Seeing how the student body's voice was incorporated into the development of more on-campus dining options, parking expansions around campus, the opening of the new Blackshear Stadium, and countless other projects, made my experience in SGA worthwhile. My time as President can be put into a million words because I was provided with so many opportunities that most don't get to experience, especially coming from Ama, Louisiana.

The value of a college degree is far more than just coursework. There is a journey filled with some of life's most valuable lessons included and where men and women around the world get a chance to push themselves into the next class of the world's leaders and innovators. For me it was my first chance to see how a man can learn to navigate obstacles, find the beauty in life's challenges, and be able to show up everyday with a positive mindset. I left college with memories to last a lifetime, friends to enjoy life's beauty with forever, and a desire to make a positive lasting imprint on society, while sharing the fact that Prairie View Produces Productive People, to the world. I was able to witness President Barack Obama's 2nd Inauguration, develop bonds with people who are now family to me, see the world grow from a birds eye view, and finally gain an understanding of myself. No matter where life takes you, embrace it like its your last moment.

About Sidney LeBeauf

Sidney LeBeauf is a May 2017 Graduate of Prairie View A&M University, with a Bachelor of Science in Civil and Environmental Engineering. Sidney LeBeauf's origins start in Ama, Louisiana, a town of more than 1200 people, located about 15 miles West of New Orleans, Louisiana. Ama is a relatively small town, with a calming aura. Sidney would always dream of life outside of Ama and even the state of Louisiana. Sidney decided to attend Prairie View A&M University and study Civil Engineering, providing an opportunity to spend some time in the state of Texas and start a new chapter in life. During his time spent on The Hill, Sidney was constantly reminded that choosing Prairie View was a great decision. Since graduating Sidney has spent time in the construction management industry, working on some interesting projects over the years.

KENNETH WILSON JR.

From Legacy to Leader
Kenneth Wilson Jr.

I grew up in Dallas, Texas. My then young mother and father, left Tallulah, Louisiana to escape generational poverty to provide me, my older brother and younger sister with better opportunities.

I attended summer programs growing up, like the Boys and Girls Club, and I started playing organized sports in middle school. I worked hard after being cut from the basketball team in seventh grade, only to get picked up the following season. By playing basketball three times a day at the Boys and Girls Club, I made the varsity basketball team my first year at Richardson High School. I also liked the high jump and long jump in Track & Field.

My parents decided to move back to Louisiana after my junior year, when my grandfather passed away. My mother did not want my grandmother to be alone, but she allowed me to move in with a friend to finish out my senior year of high school. That was the best decision for me. I am forever thankful that she trusted that I could be responsible while they moved a whole state away!

As fate would have it, I went on to receive a full Track & Field scholarship to attend Prairie View A&M University, where I wanted to study Mechanical Engineering. I did not know how difficult the road to accomplish this would be, but I kept my faith in the Lord and myself. I trusted the process. My family came to town to watch me graduate high school. It was such an amazing feeling! After graduation, my parents drove me back to Louisiana to spend the summer there before college. I worked at a local daycare and could not wait for college to start. Summer passed quite quickly, and my parents dropped me off after we made the drive from Tallulah, LA to Prairie View A&M University.

I worked hard to earn and keep my scholarship, despite injuries. I still excelled in engineering by overcoming the time management challenges. I worked hard in both avenues and gained awards such as the Dean's list award and the University Honors award for earning a 3.8 GPA. I also made the all-academic Track & Field team several years. By my senior year of college, I was a campus leader, serving as Director of Social Action for Phi Beta Sigma Fraternity, Incorporated. I won an award for best seminars in the state of Texas, and I won seven Track & Field conference medals: three bronze, three silver, and one gold, along with three championships rings!

Pledging was quite an experience. It opened many doors for me. I am thankful for all that I learned at Prairie View A&M University. One great lesson is that I learned how to say, "Yes!" to opportunities that made a difference and say, "No!" to distractions while striving to achieve my goals.

After pledging Phi Beta Sigma, I landed a fall Co-op where I worked for Caterpillar in Peoria, Illinois. I had a 3.51 GPA at the time and just needed to get an internship under my belt. Days after I crossed, I added Phi Beta Sigma to my resume the night before the career fair. A high school friend told me to stop by and speak to Caterpillar. Refusing to miss class, I knew they were going to have an informational session about the company at the National Society of Black Engineers meeting. I got there early to get a good seat so I could be the first to speak to the presenters after it was over. Immediately after the session was over, I grabbed my notes and was the first to talk to Michael Mosley. I gave him my elevator speech. As he skimmed over my resume, he gave me the Sigma grip. I knew then that I was in good hands. Weeks later, I had a phone interview, which I completed in the comfort of my room, which led to an offer for a paid Co-op.

While working as a filter engineer, I became green belt certified. I did this while pressure testing spin on filters in the lab. I did not have anything to work on one day, so I went back to my engineering manager Jeff for more work. I picked up a task called muffler consolidation that I was not expected to finish since it had over 1,000 mufflers. Since I wanted to make a great impression, I planned out how many I would have to finish before my Co-op was over. I went to work early some days, finished early and blew them away!

That green belt certification opened the door for me to work as a mechanical intern at BNSF Railway in Kansas City, Kansas the next summer. This company paid me a little more, but they also gave me a housing stipend of $500 a month. I was able to find an apartment to rent for $535. So, essentially, my rent was only $35 dollars. I had been saving for a car since my freshman year. I worked two jobs that summer and purchased my first car. I was very passionate about my summer internship. I lived out on the shop floor and had a relationship with the workers. One day, one of the workers asked me if I had ever been on a train before. I hadn't. So, they had me come aboard and I was very excited. I took a few photos with my camera to capture the moment. An engineer told me they had finished fixing that train and were about to move it. He asked me, "Do you want to drive this train?"

"Yes!" I replied, emphatically. That day, I was afforded the opportunity to drive a train.

That summer was one for the history books. I loved the feeling of driving from Kansas City, Kansas back to Texas in my new car. I am thankful for the family atmosphere I gained from attending Mt. Corinth Baptist Church in Heavenly Hempstead and the close relationships that I formed with my track team, specifically Coach Gilliard. Taking nineteen credit hours, filled with all engineering classes, during the fall semester of my senior year, I talked to Coach Gilliard before the season started. I realized that I needed to focus, and I would not be able to make it to practice that semester. Concerned about what my coach might say, Coach Gilliard responded, "Get your lesson fessor," which was a short compliment for professor. Coach Gilliard allowed me to keep my full scholarship, and he would allow me to keep running Track & Field during my graduating spring semester. I was a part of winning two championship rings that semester.

Prairie View A&M University opened many doors for me during that stressful semester. I landed countless interviews. I flew to Eagan, Minnesota, Atlanta, GA, and Florida to interview for various full-time careers. Being recognized as a campus leader, I was also selected to fly to Manhattan, NY, where I was handpicked to introduce a keynote speaker at the Thurgood Marshall Leadership Conference. I attended my first Broadway show, *The Color Purple*, during that trip and met several celebrities.

After my HBCU experience, I went on to become an international engineer, having recruited engineers at the NSBE conference in Toronto, Canada. Months later, I flew into London to work in Derby, United Kingdom for Rolls Royce headquarters for three weeks. About six months later, I lived and worked in Berlin, Germany, while working for Rolls Royce Deutschland for two months. During my years at Lockheed Martin, I worked on the ERAM program, which provides the software to monitor planes in domestic airspace! ERAM was created to prevent another September 11 or an airplane that goes missing, like the Malaysian airliner. After serving in the U.S. Navy as a fighting Seabee, I completed graduate school and received various offers to work for NSWC Crane. I accepted an offer to work as a manufacturing engineer, which is my current position and relocated my wife and son there in April of 2021.

About Kenneth Wilson Jr.

Kenneth D. Wilson Jr is a servant leader that grew up in Dallas Texas. He went on to receive a full track & field scholarship to attend Prairie View A&M university, where he studied Mechanical engineering. Despite hardships, Kenneth worked hard in both avenues and gained awards like the Dean's list, university honors for earning a 3.8 GPA and made the all-academic track and field team several years. By senior year, Kenneth was a campus leader: serving as Vice President of Pi Tau Sigma, the international mechanical engineering honor society, director of social action selected to plan and hold seminars on campus for Phi Beta SIGMA fraternity incorporated, where he won an award for best seminars in the state of Texas.

Kenneth is an international engineer, having worked in Derby, United Kingdom for Rolls Royce headquarters and he lived and worked in Berlin, Germany for Rolls Royce Deutschland for two months.

During his 3 years at Lockheed Martin, he worked on the ERAM program which provides the software to monitor planes in domestic airspace! ERAM is a critical program, needed to ensure that there will never be another 11 September or an airplane that goes missing like the Malaysian airliner. After serving in the US Navy as a fighting Seabee, he completed graduate school at North Carolina A&T State University and received four offers to work for NSWC Crane. He accepted an offer to work as a manufacturing engineer in 2020 and currently holds a Department of Defense Secret Clearance.

Kenneth began motivational speaking in 2010. One year after he completed local Toastermaster's International training while working at Lockheed Martin, he took a week-long public speaking class. Since that time, he has had various opportunities to speak at colleges, high school's and even volunteers to read at elementary schools.

DESMOND SHIEF

The College Experience
Desmond Shief

Resilience, determination, and self-discipline are the words that come to mind when I think about my college experience. Being the first one in my household to decide to attend college was an excessively big step for me. I had my mind set on going to Sam Houston State University; however, after going on a college tour field trip with my high school, my decision quickly changed. We toured the campus of Prairie View A&M University and immediately, I was embraced by the rich culture, history, and traditions of the school. I had no knowledge of what a Historically Black College was until I stepped foot on the campus where I was informed of the meaning and purpose of these institutions. I can honestly say that the decision to attend Prairie View was one of the best decisions I've made in my life.

Prairie View A&M University is located in Prairie View, Texas, about forty-five minutes outside of Houston. The campus was founded in 1876 as "Alta Vista Agricultural and Mechanical College of Texas for Colored Youth." It is a land grant institution and is listed in the Texas constitution along with Texas A&M University. I have so much love and respect for my HBCU and the impact that it made on my life. I will forever be indebted to my school. It made me who I am today. It's the reason I chose a career in education by teaching the youth and making an impact on the next generation.

There's no school like PV—from Fried Chicken Mondays to Catfish Fridays, from Springfest to Homecoming, and just the energy of being on "The Hill" is unmatched. I pride myself on graduating from an HBCU but graduating from Prairie View A&M University sets me apart from the rest. We would chant, "PVU is the place to be, and it ain't never gon' stop" every time we played sports and another school came to the yard. We screamed from the top of our lungs anytime we scored, and the band played our anthem.

I embarked upon my collegiate career in fall 2013, majoring in criminal justice with a minor in African American studies. I had no clue of the trials that came with being in college, along with being the first person in my family to attend a four-year university. I had to change my outlook on school and who I was as a person. The journey took off quickly and learning to adapt to this situation was challenging. During my freshmen year, I allowed distractions to influence me where my focus shifted, and my GPA reflected my poor decisions. As the winter break approached, I was placed on academic probation and had to write an appeal to the financial aid department to keep receiving funds. Going through that situation motivated me to change my mindset on how I needed to maneuver going forward. The following spring semester, I got involved on campus by joining organizations, I changed my study habits, and I didn't miss class. Being in college gave me freedom that I did not have prior to, which I took advantage of in the wrong way. Class wasn't a priority for me when it is the *main* priority.

Despite the challenges that I faced in the beginning, I can't deny the great times that I did have during my freshmen year, along with the bonds I formed with people who are now lifelong friends. I lived in University College, the freshmen dorms where all the buildings were separated by gender. The group of friends I made that year was always together. We created memories that will last a lifetime. We began to hold each other accountable, set goals, and encouraged each other to not give up while we were in school. Many people who never attended college may not understand the struggles and hardships someone goes through while trying to matriculate through undergraduate years. From hungry days to sleepless nights studying for final exams, it can be difficult on one who's unprepared to go through. Some days, I had no clue how I got through the day; but I didn't allow myself to get in my own way. So, I pushed through.

As I continued through school, I took an interest in a particular fraternity that I've known I wanted to be a part of since high school. Greek life at PV was a major thing, especially to impressionable young adults whose family consisted of members of those organizations. I started to make myself known by joining campus organizations such as Student Government Association, and Criminal Justice Club. I was also a campus tour guide and I worked for the recruitment and marketing departments. These organizations allowed me to gain a work ethic that would take me far beyond college. I eventually joined the best fraternity known to man—Kappa Alpha Psi Fraternity, Inc., after I graduated from college through a graduate chapter. Becoming a member of this fraternity was another great accomplishment that I had looked forward to for years.

Prairie View has influenced my life in so many ways, even to this day. It has created so many opportunities for me. I've traveled to so many places that I probably wouldn't have gone had I not attended Prairie View—school trips to New York for the *Macy's Thanksgiving Day Parade*, trip to D.C. for the opening of the National Museum African American History and Culture, and to Atlanta to witness our band, "The Marching Storm" compete in the *Battle of the Bands*. It's no doubt that I will continue to be the person that Prairie View produced in the spring of 2018. My experiences at Prairie View are priceless. I am grateful for it and for the people who I met along my journey in college. HBCUs are essential to African Americans more so now than ever before. I am truly an advocate for going to Historically Black Colleges.

About Desmond Shief

Desmond Shief, born in New Orleans, LA July 23, 1995. Due to Hurricane Katrina I was relocated to Houston, Tx. in 2005 where I attended high school and graduated from Nimitz Senior High School. In the spring of 2018, I graduated from the prestigious Prairie View A&M University with my bachelor's degree in Criminal Justice and a minor in African American studies. During my time at the university I was involved in numerous organizations such as Criminal Justice Club, Student Government Association, mentoring organizations, campus tour guide and recruiter. My passion for my HBCU led me to become an advocate for historical black schools. Currently, I am an educator for Idea Public Schools where I am the Accelerated Reading facilitator. I joined the greatest fraternity known to man Kappa Alpha Psi Fraternity, Inc. in the spring of 2020.

ANDREW HOOEY

Cultivating Creativity
Andrew Hooey

Due to the fact that my family experienced so much history at Prairie View A&M University, it was only befitting for me to begin my journey at this beautiful HBCU. Majority of both my mother's side and father's side attended Prairie View. As a senior in high school, I wasn't sure which college I wanted to attend. I applied to multiple colleges; however, apparently my mother only wanted me to go to Prairie View—so much so that she threw away the acceptance letters I received from other universities. I ended up choosing (or not) to attend Prairie View, and it was literally the best decision I could have made.

An HBCU experience is one of a kind. It is an experience that you will not get anywhere else. The best way I can describe it is that when you are in corporate America, you may be labeled as "the Black guy/girl"; but at an HBCU, you are just *you*. The history of Prairie View influenced so many facets of my life. Despite still having PTSD from standing in the financial aid line, attending Prairie View helped influence my problem solving and creative thinking.

At the start of my freshman year at PV, I remembered my mom and dad telling me about a Church of Christ that was "on campus," but I could not find it anywhere partly because I didn't have a car). On top of that, the church wasn't exactly on campus. It was slightly off campus on Bledsoe St. at the end of the street. The church is called Prairie View Church of Christ. One day when I was in the MSC (cafeteria), I saw my future wife, D'Ann Hooey. She excitedly came to me and told me about the church that was "on campus." From then on, she offered to give me rides to church, and our friendship grew.

The minister at Prairie View Church of Christ was John Branden, who actually married my parents and would always remind me of it. I began serving at the church and Brother Branden took a favoring to me. He helped develop me into a teacher and preacher of the Word. There were times when he was grooming me, and I was completely unaware of it. I preached every now and then. Throughout my time there, I grew in my craft. I started an organization on campus that was an extension of the church called Prairie View Church of Christ Organization. We offered bible studies to students every Thursday, and we had a lot of fun hosting and ministering to the students. Currently, the church is thriving. Although I'm no longer a student there, I am an active member at my current church, Highland Heights Church of Christ, where I am a ministerial student who preaches and teaches bible studies.

I majored in electrical engineering, which is a challenge to say the least. Let's just say that before I got into engineering, I used to love math; but after going through the program, *I hate it!* I'm just kidding, but there are parts of math that are not for me. Engineering taught me the importance of teamwork. There were classes that I excelled at on my own, and there were also classes where I had no idea what was going on. That's when I had to rely on my friend's group to help pull me through. If you are a student looking to major in engineering, know that you can accomplish things quickly if you do it alone, but you can accomplish more if you do it with your team.

My freshman year I was involved in NSBE, National Society of Black Engineers. Through this organization, I obtained an internship every year as a student, and received my full time offer from Exxon before graduation. Staying involved and taking action even when I didn't know everything I was doing helped me in this sense. While studying for engineering tests every other week, I ran for and won the title of homecoming king of the university four years in a row and became first runner up to Mr. Prairie View in my fifth year. (Shout out to my mother, Coy Hooey who was so supportive in getting me the flyers and candy I needed.) Looking back the networking and relationship building from this experience has served me so much in my life.

Currently, I work as entrepreneur at a mortgage company where we serve PV Alumni along with others in purchasing homes. The immense amount of organization, communication, time management, relationship building has been my key to success. My drive and work ethic has set me apart from others in the industry because I prioritize my time and give my clients the necessary attention they deserve. I learned how to become the muse needed for the occasion while avoiding self-serving activities. I focused on what I can do to increase a client's confidence while going through the process. I perfected home qualifying; my mentality has always been "anything for the client." In the same respect, mortgages are all about aligning clients with the best loan program that allows them to achieve their goals. I learned to step outside of the traditional ways of financing to capture the bigger picture and understand what the end goal is for each client.

The journey here was not easy. There have been failures, doubt, lessons and hurdles; but for me, it's not about what happens to you. What matters is how you respond to the adversity. My mindset on life it to value your that life isn't promised to anyone, so love them today, forgive, don't stress over things that aren't in your control. If you know me, then you know I never meet a stranger and my heart is full of love, joy, and excitement.

I thank God because without him, I wouldn't be here. I met my wife, D'Ann Hooey while attending Prairie View so if nothing else was gained, all was worth it in meeting her. She has been a great support and spiritual influence on me. I thank my parents, Coy and Reginald Hooey, my sister Kiki Hooey and my brother David Hooey for supporting me throughout my journey.

Many people think that college and formal education are timewasters. I can understand why they say that, but there is immense value that you get from the network that an HBCU brings into your life. And although there are many classes that you don't ever use again, what you will always use is the discipline and creativity it cultivates in you, especially with approaching different problems. I wouldn't exchange my experience at Prairie View for anything in the world and plan to send my children there one day.

About Andrew Hooey

Andrew Hooey is a proud Houston native and Prairie View Alumni who graduated in 2016 with a bachelor's in Electrical Engineering. He believes in putting his best foot forward in all he does. As a lover of God he focuses his energy on living in his purpose, helping others, and giving back to the community.

Andrew may very well be the most competitive person you'll ever meet, which allowed him to win homecoming king 4yrs in a row while he was a student at Prairie View and was first runner up to Mr. Prairie View in his final year. After graduating, he secured employment with the number one Oil and Gas Company in the world and now is a Branch Manager at a Black Owned Mortgage Company where he offers his clients quality service and interest rates for home purchases and refinances.

NA'SHON EDWARDS, SR.

Lean Not On Your Own Understanding

Na'Shon Edwards, Sr.

January 8, 2012, 6:07 PM

This date and time will forever be etched in my heart. On this day, I received my letter of acceptance to the best HBCU in the land. At that point, I didn't know much about Prairie View A&M University and honestly, I didn't care to know. I understood that this university was my key to success and a chance to move out of my hometown of Beaumont, Texas.

My journey at PV began in the summer of 2012 through a then pilot summer bridge program called Panther Pride. This five-week program was designed for first-year students to receive college credits before starting their first year. Fresh out of high school, I was ready to show my peers who I thought I was. That summer was filled with joy, blessing, and all-around entertainment, thanks to University College staff. That summer was serious because it ultimately set the pace for my academic career at PVAMU going into the fall semester. I felt like I was on the top of the world when I finished the summer semester with a 3.5 GPA. I made many new friends and was able to say that I was in college. The world was truly mine—at least for that moment.

My fall semester as a freshman started off well. Classes were where I wanted them, financial aid was locked in, and I had my tickets to the Labor Day Classic—my first collegiate HBCU football game. *How could this not get any better?* I thought.

September 5, 2012, 4:11 PM

On this day, my attitude concerning life, education, and perseverance changed forever. I was living off-campus, which was a "no-no" because typically, first-year students were still trying to figure out the lay of the land in terms of university services and routines. Nevertheless, I wanted to be "grown," so I decided to move off Texas Highway 6 near Cypress, Texas. A major mistake. Although it was cool to live so far from campus during my first full year of college, it ultimately was one of the many straws that could have broken my back.

September 5th seemed like the longest day ever. I went from having my own vehicle and space to being displaced and carless in a matter of hours. The expectation was to maintain a decent GPA and go to class. Adulthood was at my front door, and decisions had to be made: should I go home or fight it out one day at a time? I chose the latter because I knew that my story was not written or told—at least not yet. With the decision to stay in school, I learned how to get uncomfortable with my image and ego. Moreover, I had to get comfortable with asking for help. By the end of my freshman semester, I'd slept at more parks and showered at more gyms than I can remember. I'd worn the same three shirts and two pairs of pants and walked my penny loafers down to my socks. It was challenging, and I finished my first semester with a 1.6 GPA. Hurt wasn't the word to describe how I felt because I forgot to remove the high expectation that I had on myself. I had to remember to give myself some grace, given the circumstances. That's when my beloved PVAMU family stepped in and turned my life around.

I spoke with my advisor, Ms. Phyllis Spates about my life and semester. I was broken and needed so much help. I finally broke down and told her everything that happened, and the rest was history. She connected me with Ms. Vivian Dorsett, who was over the university's foster home students' program. She connected me with a family of students who accepted me and never turned their back on me. Ladarius Jones was the upperclassman who took me in without question and let me stay on the couch. I was appreciative and made a vow to pay it forward someday to somebody. Now that I was in a stable environment, I was closer to the university, had resources that enabled me to work on campus and boosted my GPA to a 3.4! I knew many who shared a similar story and couldn't bounce back into their sophomore years. That's why that portion of my story must be told. I learned so much and had to grow up fast if I expected to graduate or even be successful in my own right. Going into my sophomore and junior years, I committed to getting more involved on campus and finally creating some foundation for myself.

The organization that boosted my development as a student and person was Brother 2 Brother, spearheaded by the late Daryl Williams. I looked forward to Tuesday afternoons because we met for an hour to discuss what was going on in our lives as young, Black men. It was a space where you felt welcomed and heard. There were no positions, no hierarchy—just dialogue and the yearning to be heard and seen by my peers. My commitment to this cause opened many doors for me to lead in the space that required mentorships, such as serving as president of Black and Brown Brothers (B3CUBD), vice president of Men of Vision, and Inaugural Class of MALE. While serving in these spaces, I learned the power of respect, intentionality, and professionalism in the academic space. I was proud to be a member of organizations meaningful to my mission as a man and an emerging leader on campus.

One day during a service event on campus, I received an invitation to be on the Student Government Association Food Service Committee, the student-led committee over the Sodexo quality of food. This was my first introduction to social circles, politics, and institutional leadership. Being a part of those decision-making meetings truly opened my eyes to how things work. Long story short, I quickly rose through the ranks of the Executive Branch by serving as the vice president of Business Affairs in 2015, chief of staff in 2016-17, and advisor to the President in 2017-2018. I must say that my proudest moments came in 2016-2017 because of three major projects that solidified my legacy on the campus.

The first project spearheaded a blackface incident involving one of the student-athletes during an away game. While the student-athletes were on their way back to campus, the news of the incident spread like wildfire, and the students wanted to know how leadership would address this. Long story short, then SGA President Jacolahn Dudley held a forum for student leaders to develop an idea for remediation. Mr. Kendric Jones, the SGA Comptroller, started the meeting with a quote from Martin Luther King, Jr., "Only light can drive out the darkness, and only love can drive out hate." That struck a chord with me, and I drew the concept for a Love + Light unity photo on the brand-new football stadium. I worked for about two hours to knock this out, but ultimately it was a success thanks to members of SGA, the Marching Storm Band, and the student body.

The last two projects are in tandem. The second project is the formation of the Prairie View A&M University Ring Committee, which redesigned the PVAMU ring and put resources behind the ring's marketing. The third project is the revamping of the university's graduation regalia, which is what you see today. The ring and regalia projects were worthwhile because they allowed people to boldly showcase our beloved university from a new, fresh lens. Every time I see a graduate walk across the stage or meet an alum with their university ring, I am humbled because I would not have been here if I didn't keep my aspirations high and faith in God.

As I close, Prairie View has genuinely been great to me in terms of my career and family. I was fortunate enough to meet my wife on the campus of PVAMU. My mother-in-law was my professor in the summer of 2016. I saw her daughter but figured that she was out of my league. But look at me now! Six years and one son later! It's been joyous. Lastly, I had the privilege of starting my political career at PVAMU by running for Prairie View City Council as a junior. Although I didn't win, the political bug bit me, and I haven't looked back ever since. I have been a part of several fellowships in Austin, Houston, and Washington, D.C. Now, I serve as the director of constituent services for Houston City Council, District F and co-founder of Edwards and Jones Consulting in Houston, Texas. Prairie View A&M University has been too good to me, and I owe it to the PVAMU, which is why I will always root for my alma mater.

About Na'Shon Edwards, Sr.

Na'Shon Edwards, Sr., MCD is a doctoral student at Liberty University majoring in Public Policy with an emphasis in Social Policy. As a graduate student at Prairie View A&M University in 2017, Na'Shon, Sr., has committed his research effort to Community Development Research and Policy in rural and urban regions in Texas. Na'Shon, Sr. currently serves as the Director of Constituent Services & Housing Research for Houston City Council District F under Councilmember Tiffany D. Thomas. Na'Shon, Sr.'s work has been presented through academic organizations such as the Community Development Society, American Research Education Association, Community Development Education Symposium. Lastly, he is published in the Texas Institute for the Preservation of History and Culture and the Houston Forward Time. He aspires to become a thought leader in Public Policy, emphasizing Community Development. Na'Shon, Sr., is the proud husband to MiSchelle and Na'Shon, II.

BRANDON THOMAS

H.B.C.U. (He's Breaking Curses Unexpectedly)
Brandon Thomas

P-V-UUUU Know! This is a chant coined by the "Productive People Produced" at The Prairie View A&M University. This cry out can be heard anytime the PV family gets together. The phrase never gets old, because this is just one tradition that demonstrates that we were bred to bleed purple and gold!

When I was in high school, I knew I wanted to go to college and major in civil engineering. I've always loved to design and build things. I felt God Himself put it on my heart to become an engineer. In elementary school, I was told that I had a learning disability and speech impairment; however, I did not allow that to stop me in my quest to obtain God's promise in my life. Being blessed with a strong praying mother who recognized my gifts and nurtured them, she battled the school district and forbade them to place me in special education courses. As a result of the heroic effort of my mother, I graduated from high school with honors and ranked in the high percentage amongst my peers. I was now ready to embark on my journey to my institution of higher education. I chose to attend Prairie View A&M University and major in civil engineering in August 2005. Being my first time away from home, I was ready for the freedom that comes along with being an independent male, finding his way on his own. It was time to get the college experience I had long dreamed about.

Whew! Freshman year! I remember it like it was yesterday. We eased on down Highway 290 with an SUV full of things I needed for my dorm room as well as a few items that reminded me of home. I couldn't help but feel an overwhelming sense of joy as we arrived on to "The Hill." After spending hours getting moved in, it was finally time to say goodbye to my family and start my new journey. I was a man on a mission or, at least that's what I thought. Later that evening, I attended a gathering that was organized to welcome incoming freshman to the university. It was riddled with great food, music, games and all kinds of activities to break the ice and make us feel at home. After all, this would be our home for the next four or five years.

We arrived a week early and the Welcoming Committee planned all sorts of team/bond building activities for us. During that time, I met my best friend now of seventeen years and counting. He and I immediately bonded and formed an unbreakable brotherhood that I know without a doubt will last for the duration of our lives. For me, freshman year was about building a firm foundation on networking: friendships, internships, and preparing for the future.

My matriculation at Prairie View came with a new set of challenges. I had to quickly learn about the necessity of time management; along with decision making, budgeting, networking, and work while balancing my social life. As time went on, I mastered and became quite skilled with the art of balancing my life. That's when I discovered that the shy person I had always been, was no more. I came out of my bubble more and before I knew it, I got involved in several campus activities. I joined an engineering organization; internship programs, self-help seminars and anything else I could do to better myself.

The engineering organizations helped me to chart a deeper path into my major, civil & environmental engineering. These organizations afforded me the opportunity to do cool things like design a concrete canoe, build a city, as well as a water treatment plant. Socially, I was extended an invitation which, I accepted, to participate in my first and only scholarship pageant. This pageant was hosted by the "Devastating Divas of Delta Sigma Theta" sorority on campus. My participation in this pageant drew me so far out of my comfort zone that I was struck with a sense of fear; however, I didn't let that stop me. I got on that stage and displayed my singing and speaking ability. I got totally lost in all the excitement of the moment. For the first time in my life, I had no limits and I owe it to Prairie View!

Although education is forever the focal point of every productive Panther, there is always one week on campus where the entire world stops: the infamous PV Homecoming week. Homecoming week is a festive time where the entire campus comes together as a family with mind blowing musical concerts, step shows, pep rallies, parades, tailgating, parties and the ever so popular football game, with the award-winning halftime show. The energy generated during Homecoming week is off the charts, and the memories last a lifetime. Prairie View's sports program is a spectacle to watch all around. Throughout the year, fans and students packed the baby dome and Black Shear Stadium to cheer our Panthers on to victory. Having your priorities in line was necessary when juggling the many hats of tackling work, classes, and taking exams before the fun could commence. Between hearing the band playing with excitement and or sitting in class while DJ Mr. Rogers killed the hump day, it was almost torture to be in class or at work amid the fun. This was the life of an undergraduate at Prairie View. Whether education to entertainment, the structure of growing and maturing came in to play. You had to be focused and understand you had a main goal despite the distractions. This experience makes obtaining that degree far sweeter.

In conclusion, what a life-changing experience I had at PV! I will always reflect on my learning experiences, memories and the way it helped me develop a balanced lifestyle and work ethic. Many special bonds were created with people who were once strangers. I've gained knowledge and skills, and I've developed a level of confidence that I did not know was obtainable. I was dropped off to "The Hill" as a boy and graduated as a man of high standard and principles. For that, I am forever indebted to you, Prairie View A&M University. Thank you for being My Alma Mater!

PV! UUUUUUUUUU Know!

About Brandon Thomas

Brandon Emanuel Thomas was born and raised in Houston, Texas to the proud parents of Michael Charles Thomas and Regina Renell Stubblefield-Thomas. Brandon is the middle of three children. Brandon graduated from North Shore Sr. High School, and went onto attend Prairie View A & M University where he earned a Bachelor of Science degree in Civil & Environmental Engineering. Currently, Brandon works as a Civil & Environmental Engineer in the Harris County Engineering & Architecture Department. He is a proud member of The Delta Omicron Chapter of Omega Psi Phi Fraternity in Beaumont, Texas. His favorite bible verses are Psalm 37: 23-24 and Psalm 115:14.

Brandon founded and established the Striving to Achieve New Direction Foundation (S.T.A.N.D. Inc.) in 2017 in honor of his late father Michael Charles Thomas, who passed away when he was a teenager. S.T.A.N.D. Inc. is a mentoring and maturation program for young men in the Houston and surrounding areas that will help them gain the skills and mental fortitude necessary to succeed in life. Brandon is a devout Christian and attends the Greater Emmanuel Family Worship Center, where he serves in the Men, Singles, and Music & Arts Ministries. As a part of his daily regimen, Brandon enjoys crossfit training, jogging, cycling, signing, reading, and traveling.

ANDREA DUCRE

Planted for a Purpose
Andrea Ducre

"Dear Prairie View, our song to thee we raise.
In gratitude, we sing our hymn of praise.
For mem'ries dear, for friends and recollections,
for lessons learned while here we've lived with thee…"

Born in the small country town of New Roads, Louisiana in September 1977, I was the youngest of four children. By age four, my parents separated, and I was raised by my single mother. I was that baby girl who clung to her mother and had to be pried from her arms to leave home for head start. Everyone would always say to my mom, "She's so smart; you should get her tested for the magnet school." She did, and my enrollment was promptly transferred. I spent the rest of my childhood living up to and exceeding everyone's expectations of me. I spent hours dreaming about and planning for what was next in my life. I always knew God had a plan for me but waiting for that plan to materialize took what felt like an eternity. From growing up in that green shotgun house on Railroad Avenue to the Hills of Prairie View A&M University to study chemical engineering to now working as a people development manager at a prestigious chemical company, my development and maturity into the person I am today started and was solidified at PV.

In May 1995, I graduated high school as a co-Salutatorian along with my best friend, Letitia, since third grade. I was awarded a full academic scholarship to PVAMU with all out-of-state fees waived. What a blessing. That same summer, I left my job at Dairy Queen on the beautiful banks of False River to start my collegiate career in the Engineering & Science Concepts Institute (ESCI) summer program. Although I was the first in my immediate family to attend college, my older cousin, Nicole, had graduated from Prairie View. She was a huge inspiration and one of the main reasons why I ultimately chose to attend PV. She finished years earlier in civil engineering. Thankfully, my Aunt Marilyn and her family were also nearby in Missouri City if I needed a lifeline.

The first summer experience was priceless. That was my time to explore the campus, figure out college life, and get a head start before the true freshmen joined in August. The pace was slower, but the work was challenging. Coming from a small rural town in Louisiana, my only knowledge of college life was what I had seen on television watching *A Different World*, along with my summers staying on Southern University's campus for the Upward Bound Program. My highest level of math education was advanced math at Pointe Coupee Central. When I made it to PV, many of my classmates had completed calculus in high school. That's when the fear, doubt, and questions crept in: *Can I do this? Do I belong here? Will I be able to keep my scholarship and make my family proud?* Nevertheless, instead of cowering to fear, I put my head down and got to work. I asked for help when I needed it and learned how to study effectively. By the end of that semester of calculus with Dr. Frazier, I was awarded a plaque for the highest GPA in the class. That solidified everything for me; I belonged, and I could do it.

Academics at PV continued to be interesting and challenging even before starting engineering classes. Who could ever forget freshman composition with Dr. B.J. Freeman and her African headdress and philosophical discussions or evening Honors Colloquium lectures? I vividly remember reciting my final on Maya Angelou in speech class. The research and knowledge gained about Ms. Angelou were life-changing and inspirational.

Some of my fondest memories of campus life were having dinner with friends in Alumni and taking our evening walks. We would take a stroll to the post office to check our mail, praying to receive a letter from home, a high school friend, or maybe even a phone card. Those evenings, we could hear the band practicing in Hobart Taylor, getting ready for the weekend's performance. We always loved those tantalizing beats. Unlike most, who gained "the freshman 15," I managed to lose weight freshman year. I believe leaving DQ, no longer eating my 10 p.m. banana splits along with being on a fully pedestrian campus contributed to this accomplishment.

There is no place like an HBCU. The experiences and lifelong friendships gained foster and change the trajectory of your life. Watching on-campus step shows in front of the bookstore as you watch to see who is coming out Greek was always exciting. The music, energy, and vibes on campus were addictive. In the back of all the engineering students' minds was how much time can I stay before I need to leave and get some work done (always remembering the priorities). Campus game days were good, too. Plan for enough time to get to half time for the band's performance. We were on campus during the era of no winning games, so we had to find joy in other aspects of the game-day experience before heading back to Drew Hall or The Village Phase I.

In spring 1997, I went with some friends to a "meeting." Following that day, my life was forever changed, as I was joined to eighteen others as the 19 Degrees of Separation in Epsilon Gamma Iota Engineering Coed Fraternity. Physics II & the Lab were experienced differently by those online at that time. I am forever indebted to Reagan for her support through it all. Lifelong memories and friendships were formed during that semester. Even now, Niecy continues to entertain me while reminiscing about the good ole days coupled with hour-long conversations about life.

Overpayment checks and scholarship dollars gave me some financial support during those years. I was the true definition of a broke college student. I managed to get my first internship in the summer of 1997 in Pasadena. I was able to live with my Aunt Marilyn and earn enough money to purchase my first car. I felt freedom and the weight of the responsibility that came with debt. I learned to budget and save enough that summer to sustain me until the next internship.

The remainder of that year and the year following tested me, my strength, and my resilience. I made mistakes, lost friends, lost my seven-year-old niece to sickle cell anemia, and lost my maternal grandmother. I realized that not everyone who comes into your life is there for a lifetime. Some are only for a season. God is always preparing you for the next chapter. I now realize that I was just planted at the time to draw nearer to Him.

During the summer of 1998, I had another internship in Freeport and found space to work on myself. I also bonded and grew a deeper friendship with my college best friend, or EEBFF (Extra, Extra Best Friend Forever), as my godson calls her. Although Shon and I had crossed paths before, that summer was our time to connect and solidify a relationship that will prove to survive decades. To meet a person with such a kindred spirit to you was truly like having a sister from another mother. We studied together late while Shon survived on NoDoz. We also spent time together walking, talking, or just sitting as we introverts do. We were in the same senior design group, so we were connected not just for the friendship, but also to complete the degree we came to PV in pursuit of.

I graduated from PVAMU on May 8, 1999, magna cum laude in chemical engineering with multiple job offers. I have been forever grateful for the experiences gained. Preparing for career fairs, stressing the importance of internships and extracurricular activities, and maintaining my GPA versus trying to recover it were instilled in me from the start. All the tips, advice, and information shared by all those who went before me ordered my steps on this journey.

While at Prairie View, I saw the world change before my eyes. The World Wide Web connected us for the first time, we started carrying cell phones (with rollover and roaming minutes), police chases and court cases played out on live television, and tragic school shootings became a reality.

Through it all, PV has been my ever-evolving constant. Every drive along Highway 290 is a trip down memory lane. Remembering how things were in the mid-nineties compared to what I see today, things are forever growing and progressing. For any trip, whether for homecoming, career fairs, interviews, or just because, I am reminded each time I cross the flag poles and see the majestic library just ahead that Prairie View produces productive people, and I am proud to be a part of that elite club.

Dear Prairie View, you will forever be knitted in the fabric of my heart and soul.

About Andrea Ducre

Andrea Battley Ducre is a native of New Roads, Louisiana, and a resident of Baton Rouge. After graduating in Chemical Engineering from Prairie View in 1999, she joined ExxonMobil Chemical Company. Over the last 22 years, Andrea has worked in various engineering and supervisory roles at three of ExxonMobil's Baton Rouge chemical manufacturing facilities. Her experience has primarily been in polymers. She is currently serving as the Baton Rouge Area People Development Manager. In this role, she is coaching early-career engineers and their supervisors/managers to play an active role in developing diverse talent. She also supports the implementation of the Inclusion and Diversity strategy for the area. While at ExxonMobil, Andrea has been a part of multiple PV campus recruiting teams that attend the annual career fairs and campus interviews to continue to bring talented engineers into the company.

Andrea is a busy professional, wife, and mom. She has been married to Edward for nearly twelve years. Together they have three children, Sierra, Edward, Jr., and Dylan. Andrea is also the primary caregiver for her mom, Betty, and her niece with special needs, Dabrielle. She and her family are members of Healing Place Church. When Andrea is not working or caring for her family, she can be found riding her spin bike, watching football, baking, or reading /studying God's word.

SHARON CARTER BLAIR

Feels Like Home
Sharon Carter Blair

"Prairie View A&M University!"

I will never forget the first time I heard those words! I was in the counselor's office at South Oak Cliff (SOC) High School when my counselor mentioned that there was a scholarship for a summer program and to attend Prairie View A&M University right after graduation. I told my mother about it, and she said, "That is where you are going to go." Of course, in my mind, I was like, "Oh, no I am not!" My mind was made up; I was going to UT-Austin. I had been accepted there and that was the big school I wanted to attend, no matter what I had to do.

"No. Prairie View is where you need to be so that you can learn and be with your own kind," my mom responded. I knew what she meant by this, but I was happy no matter where I went to school. I loved school and learning. Changing schools was the norm growing up, and I adjusted the best I could.

I've always known that I would attend college, but I never knew where I would go. I graduated from South Oak Cliff High School in Dallas, Texas in May 1982. Just a couple of weeks after, I was at Prairie View A&M University.

Born in Shreveport, Louisiana, the only Historically Black College and University that I had heard of at the time was Grambling State. My mother's first cousin attended Grambling and the band marched in the Christmas parades in downtown Shreveport. It was always exciting to see them perform, and I wanted to be around that excitement!

Being in a military family (my dad and stepdad were in the Army), moving was part of the business. I attended numerous elementary and junior high schools during my early years. In 1978, my family moved to Dallas, Texas. I attended several high schools before winding up at South Oak Cliff for my junior and senior years. Before this point, I had always attended schools that were predominately white. I liked SOC and thought I adjusted well to the culture of the school. I just didn't know a lot about the other students because they had attended school together from elementary to high school and/or they grew up in the same neighborhood.

Attending Prairie View A&M University was one of the best decisions that my mom and I made! I learned a lot about myself and the traditions, and I loved the atmosphere. One thing that I learned about myself was that it was okay to change your mind and not be so rigid. Some classes were difficult, and I had to decide if I wanted to continue in my chosen major. I changed my major halfway through school. I was making an adult decision and was going to be responsible for others regardless of my career choice. Later in life, I changed my career focus because my life changed when I had my daughter. She was born with special needs, so I had to fight and speak up for her medical and education needs.

I earned my BBA in Accounting, and my graduate degree is in Social Work with a school concentration. My choices for careers were total opposites, but I enjoyed them. However, taking care of my "rugrat" was more important. To this day, I am still a person who is rigid and needs a schedule, but I've learned to be more flexible and consider my options.

I was the first-generation college graduate in my immediate family. One of my high school teachers, Ms. Turner, told me about her college experiences, but I did not know what to expect. The first time I saw Prairie View, a few of us rode down with my friend Carla and we traveled on the back roads to get to campus. Prairie View was about four hours from Dallas. *Where in the world was this school?* I wondered. Once we got to campus and in front of Drew Hall, there was a mixture of old and a little new. I felt like I was in the middle of nowhere and back in the past simultaneously.

In the fall, Drew Hall was where all of the upperclassmen congregated to see the new freshman—mainly girls. I had never seen that before. We rode the Greyhound Bus home, or someone was always driving home on the weekend. We walked everywhere on campus. When it rained, the red dirt turned to mud, and we walked on cardboard boxes to get to class. We used to walk to the flag poles and sit after going to the store to get Blue Bell ice cream. You saw your friends pledging as we moved up and wondered what the fraternities and sororities were all about. Step shows were always fun to see, and homecoming meant concerts, the Ms. Prairie View pageant and the end of the football season. The food at Alumni Hall was edible and decent, depending on what day it was. We had to be careful at night walking on campus because around some buildings, big bugs came out at night. Guys could only visit in the lobby at the dorms until the rules changed a few years later. Everybody used to watch *General Hospital* in the lobby of the dorm.

There were so many clubs and organizations on campus. Many groups were focused on helping students (professional/career organizations) and giving back to the surrounding communities. That's where I learned the importance of giving back to your community—speaking up for what is right, discovering that it takes time for change to happen and that there are many ways to implement change. I participated in my hometown organization and the professional organization for my major. We also were able to vote on the Permanent University Fund which is how Prairie View began receiving funds for the improvement of the school, buildings and education in the late eighties.

Over the years, giving back was, and continues to be one of my focuses. I became a school social worker. I participated in the local school councils in Chicago at two of the schools my daughter attended. Choosing a principal and voting on how to use funds for the students were important, especially in schools where the children had different special needs. My husband and I also served on the Parent Advisory Board at the University of Chicago's Comer Children's Hospital.

I continue to have lifelong friendships and bonds that were formed while attending Prairie View. Some of these people I met through my husband who also graduated from Prairie View. I have stayed connected with and visited friends from high school who also attended PV. My husband and I have stayed connected and have visited with several families in Prairie View and Hempstead, Texas for well over thirty years now. Some say family is when you are connected by blood; however, these families are not family by blood, but they are my PV family.

In fact, I met my husband at Prairie View. Some of my friends attended college to find a spouse, but that was not my intent. I came for an education. Little did I know that I would be one of the first of my friends to get married. My husband, Maurice, graduated in 1986 with a BS in Industrial Technology. He is smart, innovative and has a crazy sense of humor. We have been married and living in Chicago for the past thirty-three years. This is the longest I have ever lived in one place!

The HBCU experience is one that I could never get anywhere else! Prairie View has changed since I graduated in 1987, but when I return to campus to attend homecoming or just to visit the Houston area, the campus still feels like home. My husband and I stock up on our PV T-shirts, bumper stickers and whatever new we find. My daughter wasn't able to attend college, but she is an honorary Panther who loves tailgating at homecoming and socializing with our friends.

One lesson that I took with me from Prairie View is helping others. I advocated for my now adult daughter as she was growing up, and for the students I provided services for in my profession for the last twenty years. As I transition into retirement, I plan to continue advocating for adults with disabilities, and to find my niche in my community and help find resources for families in underserved communities.

About Sharon Carter Blair

Sharon D. Carter Blair was born in Shreveport, Louisiana. Her father and stepfather were in the Army and the family moved quite a bit. She has lived in Shreveport, Louisiana, Fort Bragg, NC, Frankfurt, West Germany, Fort Benning, Georgia, and Dallas, Texas. She has lived in Chicago, Illinois for the past thirty years.

She is a proud Golden Bear and graduate of the Class of 1982 - South Oak Cliff High School in Dallas, Texas. She attended Prairie View A&M University from May 1982 – May 1987. Graduated with a B.B.A. in Accounting in May 1987. Participated in the Dallas Club and the National Association of Black Accountants.

Pledged Alpha Pi Chi National Sorority Inc., Kappa Nu Chapter (Spring 1994) in Chicago. Proud member for over fifteen years and served as Financial Secretary and Volunteer Coordinator throughout the years.

A proud stay-at-home parent for nine years after the birth of her daughter with medical and special needs in 1993. She participated in parent groups, advisory boards, local school councils and parent panels to assist other families who were going through the process of obtaining medical and educational services for their children with disabilities.

Graduated in May 2002 with a Masters of Social Work degree with a concentration in School Social Work from the Jane Addams College of Social Work at the University of Illinois – Chicago.

Worked as a School Social Worker for ECHO Joint Agreement, a special education cooperative from 2002 until retirement in June of 2021. Advocated for and taught social skills, coping skills, etc. to students K – 8th grade. Member of ECHO IEA and Illinois Association of School Social Workers.

She has always been an avid reader of all things. She likes to travel and explore local history and cultures when visiting different places, especially Black History.

Attending an HBCU **changed** her life. Advocacy and service to community were influences while at Prairie View, throughout her life, personal and professional, and will continue to be her focus as she transitions into retirement.

JOCELYN TATUM-ADAMS

From the Mud Flats to a 3x Hall of Famer
Jocelyn Tatum-Adams

In August of 1983, Hurricane Alicia hit Houston and surrounding areas hard. I was due to report to Prairie View A&M University, but it delayed my arrival for a week. Although Prairie View was only fifty minutes away from my home, it was my first time venturing away from my close-knit family and our neighborhood, the "Mud Flats." Arriving on the campus of Prairie View A&M University on a full athletic scholarship for track & field was important for my family. I would be the first to receive a college degree, so the pressure to fulfill that dream was tremendous.

Prairie View A&M was just the extended family I needed. During the recruiting process, my legendary coach, Barbara Jean Jacket, pulled up to my home in her red convertible (that was impressive in the hood). She told my mom that I would not only excel in track and field but guaranteed me a degree. Out of 220 offers and letters received, the biggest reason I chose Prairie View A&M University was because she *stressed* family. The moment she looked directly and confidently into my mother's eyes and stated, "We will take care of your daughter," I was sold on the idea that I would conquer the world at PVAMU.

I didn't know at the time that Barbara Jean Jacket would be challenging but fulfilling. She was tough and strict; but she told me in her famous words, "Ham, you must be ten times better than your competition. PVAMU will bring that out in you, and I will make sure that you are." As I matriculated on campus, I met some amazing people during the orientation process. We didn't have the fancy computer registration we have today. I had to stand in line, punch a card for every class, and process registration. Talk about a reality check. No, this was not fun; but everyone was happy, enjoying the process and making new acquaintances simultaneously.

As we settled into Drew Hall, the brothers of Omega Psi Phi Fraternity, Incorporated greeted us. We would later learn as the "fish" on campus, that would be our first introduction to Greek life. They were kind, yet funny and scary at the same time. I would later pledge the greatest sorority ever founded for college women—Alpha Kappa Alpha Sorority, Incorporated. That experience brought me the bond of the Black college experience that you can't get anywhere else. It taught me how to use resources, work as a team, be creative and crafty at the same time, and, most importantly, serve my fellow mankind.

Those experiences reached beyond the flag poles on the Prairie View A&M University campus and has carried me throughout my life's journey. I am still an active member of my beloved sorority, and I support campus events and the University. I owe all of that to attending an HBCU. You don't leave the experience of your professors, teammates, campus community, step shows, yard shows, and hanging in front of Alumni Hall (our dining facility) as a memory once you graduate. You hold them near and dear and look forward to revisiting them every year during homecoming and other campus activities.

To be on "The Hill," you had to make do for the things you didn't have. We shared food, car rides, and anything else that you had and your roommates or suitemates (yes, six people shared a bathroom) didn't have. That was *family*. The dining hall would close between 6:00 and 6:30 p.m., and if you hadn't received your monthly ten or fifteen extra dollars or any extra from your parents, you would have to search for those extra Ramen noodles or crackers to eat late at night. Those were the good ole days. Those experiences I will always cherish. They were my sisters and most of those friends I still have today.

My experiences at PVAMU have made me the person, wife, mom, teacher, coach, and friend I am today. Prairie View A&M taught me the value of family, friendships, perseverance, grit and pride. Majoring in Health and Human Performance was a childhood dream of mine. I always wanted to teach physical education and coach. The year before I was due to graduate, Texas mandated testing certification for all teachers. I was well into my major, so changing majors or going in a different direction was not an option. The challenge to study and take a state-mandated test was hard, but that's where that "family" was further applied. My professors took their time and worked with us around the clock to be prepared. HBUCs have a vested interest in their students, so this was not even a second thought for them to help us as aspiring graduates afraid of having their graduation delayed. Running track at Prairie View A&M University and being coached by the 1992 USA Olympic Track & Field Coach Barbara Jacket taught me how to work hard, line up against anyone, and to know that I could succeed was paramount to my growth and development. We became NAIA and NCAA All Americans, conference champions, and national champions.

Prairie View A&M, a small-town university, forty-five minutes from Houston, produced athletes on a grand stage. It taught us how to be large without the necessary resources that our competitors had. We knew that if we worked hard, we would succeed. Wearing that purple and gold across our chest meant something then, and it still does to this day. The motto, "Prairie View A&M University Produces Productive People" is so evident that they took a driven, hardworking, and passionate young athletic girl and turned her into a three-time Hall of Famer in Track & Field. During my induction ceremony the only person I didn't have there that I wanted there was my mother so that she could see what her faith in me and PVAMU produced. She would have been so proud in her quiet yet shy way. She always taught us to work hard and always do what is right and good things will come from that. To my mother I say PVAMU was right and thanks for supporting my decision to attend the best HBCU in the country.

Prairie View A&M University taught me so much about family, pride, and determination. I was hired as a health & physical education teacher and coach for women's volleyball and track & field at my alma mater. I spent nine years there and amassed impressive records by winning the school's first Southwestern Athletic Conference Volleyball Championship in 1992 and was named Coach of the Year in 1990. I was probably not the most qualified when hired. Still, I had an athletic director, coach, and physical education department head who saw the drive, passion, and work ethic in me to take a chance on a young, hardworking, determined and ambitious young woman.

This is the epitome of what an HBCU experience can do. It opens an opportunity that I might not have otherwise received. I did the work, but they pushed and poured into me the tools needed to receive and accomplish the job at hand. When you are surrounded by genuine love and support, you automatically want to excel. I was moved to know the people at PVAMU cared about my growth and maturity as a student, athlete, and employee that I went on to pour those experiences into the lives of the athletes I teach and coach. I try to give them the tools they need in life. Many of my former athletes come back and thank me for not giving up on them. They say I was instrumental in them becoming teachers, coaches, nurses, and other professionals. I have personally made phone calls to other PVAMU graduates in positions that I could recommend for hire. I don't hesitate because it was done for me. This was all due to the training and tutelage from Prairie View A&M University. Dr. Mary V. White believed that I could teach, and I went on to be a campus "Teacher of the Year" and a district finalist for "Teacher of the Year" in Physical Education. Barbara Jacket believed that I could coach, and I went on to win Bi-District Championships in volleyball, conferences, and divisional championships and coached numerous All-District, All Conference, and a few Players of the Year in their respective sports.

My HBCU experience was by far the best. From the athletic contest, the socials in the small gym or as we called it, "the hot box," to the homecoming tailgates, the games, and all-night hangouts but never once losing sight that we were there for one reason, and that was to graduate with a degree from the Prairie View A&M University. Thank you, purple and gold. I am proud to be an alum and even prouder to call my experience a dream fulfilled.

About Jocelyn Tatum-Adams

Adams has coached volleyball on the collegiate and high school level. The Houston native joined Cy-Fair ISD (Cypress Springs HS) after serving nine years as head coach at Texas Southern University. Her teams won three SWAC West Divisional Championships and were conference championship runners up in 2016 and 2017. Before joining Texas Southern she was the former head coach at Eisenhower HS where her teams won back to back Bi-District Championships in 2008-2009 and 2009-2010. She was named 2008 District 19-5A Coach of the Year and District 19-5A Co-Coach of the Year.

Adams was the volleyball head coach at Prairie View A&M University from 1990-1999. In 1990 she was named SWAC Coach of Year and in 1992 her team captured the SWAC Championship Tournament title.

Adams has been recognized as a game changer for women's coaching and was presented appreciation recognition from Sigma Gamma Rho Sorority, Incorporated., the City of Houston, Mayor Sylvester Turner, Congresswoman and Congressman, Shelia Jackson Lee, and Al Green, respectively.

Adams is a member of the Prairie View A &M Sports Hall of Fame, South Western Athletic Conference (SWAC) and Texas Black Sports Halls of Fame.

Adams is married to Eric, 34 years. They are the proud parents of two daughters Erin (25) and Brooke (17).

SEAN TAYLOR

A Home Away From Home

Sean Taylor

*"Those who have no record of what their forebears have
accomplished lose the inspiration which comes from
the teaching of biography and history."*
–Dr. Carter G. Woodson[1]

As I reflect on my experiences while attending one of the most
prestigious universities in the nation, my recollection, imbued with
fond memories, beautifully reemerges. Prairie View A&M University
(PVAMU) is purely more than an academic institution. Although I
accomplished my goal of graduating with a Mechanical Engineering
degree, I strolled across PVAMU's Baby Dome graduation stage with
a package far greater than the degree I earned.

"College days swiftly pass" is a common greeting in the days leading
to graduation day, a saying that fades the further time divorces us from
college life. PVAMU's College of Engineering has a demanding
program of study that required my attention most of the time.

I spent many days and nights in the engineering lab preparing for
exams, collaborating with classmates on homework or working on
engineering projects and presentations. We regularly watched ROTC
cadets running around campus in the early hours of the day, as we
were taking a break from all-nighters completing schoolwork and
going home to get a few hours of sleep before the next class.

Fortunately for many of us engineering students, Houston, Texas'
Booker T. Washington (BTW) High School's engineering program

---

[1] Wright Edelman, Marian, *"Carter G. Woodson and Black History,"* Black Star News,
https://www.blackstarnews.com/education/education/carter-g-woodson-and-black-history-month-right-now.html, [last accessed February 14, 2022].

prepared us for the demanding coursework. BTW laid the foundation, which afforded me greater flexibility to partake in campus activities, especially during my freshman and sophomore years. Late nights talking about social justice, playing PlayStation's Madden or 007, debating a range of topics, and supporting our athletic teams during home and away games were all a part of college life. Gents, a high school service organization established in 1964 by Houston's prestigious educator and brother of Alpha Phi Alpha Fraternity, Langston Knowles, molded me into a man committed to scholarship and service. PVAMU afforded me opportunities to continue pursuing that commitment.

The fraternal experience at Historically Black Colleges and Universities (HBCUs) is unmatched. During my sophomore year, I was initiated into the Eta Gamma Chapter of Alpha Phi Alpha Fraternity. What stood out most among the brothers of the Eta Gamma Chapter was a dedication to scholarship and service—tenets I was accustomed.

"The chief significance of Alpha Phi Alpha lies in its purpose to stimulate, develop, and cement an intelligent, trained leadership in the unending fight for freedom, equality and fraternity," stated founding member Henry Arthur Callis.[2] The brothers held several leadership positions in a number of organizations on campus, from Student Government Association President, Mr. PVAMU, elected positions in several campus organizations, and leadership positions with employers on the campus.

My father preached association brings about assimilation to encourage me to surround myself with people who are doing the right things. My proximity to excellence in the brotherhood inspired me to continue moving onward and upward. Encircled around distinction, I was elected to two leadership positions in the fraternity, was a leader in math as an employed math tutor and carried

---

[2] Alpha East, "*Jewel Henry Arthur Callis*," Alpha East, https://www.alphaeast.com/history-of-alpha-phi-alpha/jewel-henry-arthur-callis/ [last accessed February 14, 2022].

leadership roles with two employers on campus. Additionally, we led volunteer activities, hosted social events and parties for the students, hosted educational forums, and even participated in a protest at the Waller County Courthouse for voting rights. We regularly participated in campus events, but scholarship and service were our utmost objective.

The university uplifted many of us and made us appreciate that we represented something greater than ourselves. As I examine the American African professionals today, I value not just the institutional training received at HBCUs, but also the unfettered ingenuity that expresses itself daily. Dr. Greg Carr, Associate Professor of Africana Studies and Chair of Afro-American studies at Howard University, wonderfully describes the importance of institutions such as HBCUs. HBCUs are unique because they provide a level of freedom experienced in far too few places.[3] We were able to serve the community, share ideas, speak freely, and educate ourselves collectively in ways I have not experienced at any other time in my life.

In addition to the beloved elders, I had the pleasure of meeting, intellectuals regularly visited the campus to speak with us. Icons such as the Grand Master Teacher and lecturer Ashra Kwesi, National Representative of the Honorable Elijah Muhammad and the Nation of Islam Minister Louis Farrakhan, poet and distinguished professor Nikki Giovanni, professor and Student Nonviolent Coordinator Committee's (SNCC) Julian Bond, community activist Quanell X, activist and professor Dr. Cornel West, and others came to educate and offer guidance. Although the university did not have a well-established Africana studies program, we regularly examined our history outside the classroom, especially prior to circa 1619. Here is where I learned that our history dates far beyond what was taught in grade school. PVAMU is where I began to understand how little I

---

[3] Cannon, Nick, "*Cannon's Class with Dr. Carr*," https://www.youtube.com/watch?v=zAEt6vw8tbs, [last accessed February 14, 2022].

knew about us and is where I acquired the research skills to begin answering questions-questions no one in my immediate family had answers for. Shout out to the sisters, brothers, and elders who helped teach knowledge of self.

The American African spiritual atmosphere saturated the campus. Early on, I had not recognized how bright the light shone. The first of its kind supported by the state of Texas in 1876, PVAMU's beginnings make it unlike most other universities in the nation and similar to other HBCUs. We walked and lived on the same grounds as our ancestors, who were enslaved on the Alta Vista slave plantation where the cotton, timber, and rice we produced helped build what is now one of the largest cities, Houston, in the U.S., both size and population.[4] In fact, PVAMU sits on one of the last strongholds of the Confederacy.[5]

I first learned about some of the rich history of PVAMU as I listened to former Prairie View mayor and Alpha Phi Alpha Fraternity brother Frank Jackson educate a body of students. Through my own research, I felt honored to walk on the same university grounds. I developed a sense of respect and duty to our ancestors. My admiration grew more as I learned about our achievements throughout the world. What a feeling of honor it was for me when I learned Dr. Jacob Carruthers, one of our most prolific scholars in the 20th century, worked as a professor on the same university grounds I walked daily.

Now, after almost a decade and a half graduating from PVAMU, I still get the colloquial butterflies when I return to the yard. Each visit reminds me how special the university—as well as other HBCUs are to the educational development of future generations.

---

[4] Michels, Patrick, "*The Interview: Frank Jackson*," https://www.texasobserver.org/prairie-view-mayor-frank-jackson-interview/, [last accessed February 14, 2022].

[5] Prairie View A&M University, "Prairie View A&M University: Celebrating 144 Years", https://giving.pvamu.edu/s/1880/bp19/interior.aspx?sid=1880&pgid=611&gid=2&cid=1540&ecid=1540&post_id=0, [last accessed February 14, 2022].

While the university continues to expand and meet tomorrow's challenges, the tightly knit bonds it fosters remain. Sankofa taught me to cherish the lengthy line of academic institutions of higher learning, like the university that "Produces Productive People."

About Sean Taylor

Sean Taylor grew up on the south side of Houston, Texas and is a descendant of the Tsogo and Ateke people who primarily reside in Gabon, Africa. Sean graduated from Prairie View A&M University in 2007 with a Bachelor of Science in Mechanical Engineering. His mother and father poured what they could into providing him early access to a good education, both private and public grade schools. As it turns out, their hard worked paid off.

During his sophomore year at Prairie View A&M University, Sean was initiated into the Eta Gamma Chapter of Alpha Phi Alpha Fraternity where he served in two elected positions and on the Step Team. His older brothers of Eta Gamma inspired Sean to expand his commitment to scholarship and service. The first book the older brothers had him read was Stolen Legacy by George G. M. James, a book that fueled his interest in his African heritage and his African family across the diaspora. His first act of service with the fraternity was feeding a family during the Thanksgiving holiday, an act of service that affixed his life's activities to the upliftment of his community. Sean was also a member of PVAMU's National Society of Black Engineers chapter where he continues its mission to positively impact the community.

Sean is an active investor in community development and educational works. He draws inspiration from icons such as Sobekneferu, Carlota Lukumi, Lucy Laney, Kwame Nkrumah, John Horse, Malcolm X, Dr. John Henrik Clarke, and countless other Greats. Today, Sean earns a living as an Information Technology professional and is the CEO and founder of a real estate investment company.

"No man can know where he is going unless he knows exactly where he has been and exactly how he arrived at his present place."
–Maya Angelou

BREIONNE BRANTLEY

The Transfer
Breionne Brantley

I will never forget the day I stood in front of John B. Coleman Library looking around at the well-manicured grass and tall bushy trees, thinking, "Thank you, God! I never thought I'd see the day I'd be here." My journey getting to Prairie View was a long one, but I made sure to stay focused and make the most of my HBCU experience.

Growing up in Blue Springs, Missouri, all of the schools I attended from fourth grade through high school were predominately white. I didn't know a lot of Black people growing up, but I knew a handful. I was the "token Black girl." I was always myself—bold, funny and outspoken. It shouldn't be a surprise to say that I was voted "Biggest Loudmouth" my senior year.

As graduation was approaching, my mother and I started looking at colleges to apply to. She told me it would be best for me to apply to an in-state college because the fees would be lower, but I knew I wanted to move to Texas. My last few summers in high school, my grandparents, Paul and Patricia Brantley, who are alumni of PV, put me in summer camps. My aunt, Dr. Mary Hawkins, also an alumna and a retired professor of PV, encouraged this as well since me and my cousins were close in age. We all participated in the STEM programs at PV, where we attended classes on campus and met other kids who ended up later attending PV.

I didn't want to pay out-of-state fees, and I had never been around predominately Black people; so, preparing for PV was going to be a challenge. I planned to apply to schools like UMKC, Northwest Missouri State, and Missouri State. Those were the schools my friends were planning to attend, but in May 2009, I graduated and decided to move to Texas, where I lived with my uncle in Dallas. To become an in-state student at PV, you must live in Texas for one year, along with a laundry list of other criteria. I enrolled at Eastfield College, where I failed during my first semester. I had a 1.7 GPA. The freedom of missing class and being in control of when I do my homework allowed me to see that I was not prepared for college. My second semester was better, but good not enough.

In the summer of 2010, I moved to DeKalb, Texas with my grandparents to attend Texarkana College. I thought being there would slow me down so I could focus on getting my GPA up. Boy, was I wrong. I did the same thing—slacked off with my classes. I was always embarrassed whenever my family asked me about school. My aunt JoAnn Brantley, who is also an alumna, told me, "You need to find a plan." That always stuck in my mind. In summer of 2011, I signed up for a certified nursing assistant class where I earned my CNA license. I worked at a nursing home and rehab hospital to save up for anything I needed to buy once I attended PV. I managed to pass all of my core classes with a B or better during my last few semesters at Texarkana College, which enabled me to apply.

In August 2012, my grandparents helped me unload and unpack my belongings in my room. I stayed in the infamous Phase 1 in building 215, room D. Shortly after getting settled, I met my first roommate, Deborah. She was one of the nicest people you would ever meet. I used to think that I was not going to like my roommate, but that was not my case. She always invited me to eat with her in the MSC. We went to all of the campus events together and enjoyed the different sororities and fraternities at "hump day" strolling. I had my eye on one sorority in particular.

Over time, I realized Deborah knew a lot of people. I will always give her credit for being the reason I knew so many people my first semester. She also had a car! That alone made my newfound college life a little easier. I also had friend from back in DeKalb, Texas named Roberto. He was going to be a freshman at PV that same semester. I used to visit him at University College, where the freshman class of 2016 was housed. He was another person who allowed me to meet so many people. Since I was in the UC often, I couldn't help but notice "the people in yellow hats." I saw them everywhere during my first semester. I spotted a guy with dreads in a yellow hat, dancing in the MSC. My roommate told me his name was "Gee." He was her friend's "PAL." I didn't know what that was, but I sure wanted to be one.

This Gee person was so full of energy. I found out later that he was the same guy in a viral YouTube video doing a PV Shuffle. I used to watch that video to get myself pumped up about going to PV. Someone told me that the people in the yellow hats were freshmen mentors, better known as "PALS," which stood for Panther Advisory Leaders. They helped guide freshmen through a successful year and gracefully transition them into their sophomore year. I wanted to be one of those people. Considering the fact that I was just a transfer student with no freshman experience, I had to wait to join the following year.

To suffice, I joined my first organization, "GMC," which stood for Gold Members Club. These were the people decked out in purple and gold who taunted opposing teams with funny chants at football and basketball games. One of Deborah's close friends was in GMC with me. We had so much fun. The most memorable moment was going to the PV vs. TSU football game at Reliant Stadium (now NRG Stadium) in Houston, Texas. Going up the escalator shouting, "MAKE MY FUNK PV FUNK, I WANTS TO GET FUNKED UP," was the most exhilarating.

In the summer of 2013, I was rewarded with a brand-new car from my grandparents after making the Dean's List the previous semester! No more depending on roommates! Right before the fall semester began, I received an email congratulating me on being chosen to be a PAL!

I went through the training process and in August, I met my assigned freshman building. I had a lively bunch of young men in building forty-six of the UC. I had the same building again in fall 2014. I loved watching these young men navigate through their freshman year. Some were popular campus DJs, won pageants, became SGA President, and joined fraternities. They really made me proud.

I participated in the Student Government Association. Many people I knew in PALs were in SGA. I didn't know exactly what I wanted to do, but I knew I wanted to be a part of positive change. I had never heard about Robert's Rules of Order or taking minutes before joining. One reward of being in SGA was the opportunity to go to different cities for a football game. I had never been to Shreveport, Louisiana or Jackson, Mississippi. There are several people I met on those trips that I am still close with to this day.

I wanted to join other organizations but wasn't sure which one. I went to an open house and learned of my options. I wanted to keep things simple by joining an organization in my major, so I signed up for the American Marketing Association, which I later became president of in fall 2014. I was also given the chance to participate in a national conference that was held in New Orleans, Louisiana. That was my first time going to the Big Easy! I learned different marketing tips that were used to assist with gaining awareness of AMA and other events happening on campus. I remember one of the members of the Eta Beta Chapter of Delta Sigma Theta Sorority, Inc. asked my organization to create a flyer for a purse drive they were doing. I created that flyer myself and had it submitted for approval. I admired this sorority so much throughout my undergraduate years. They had done so much work on campus and I was remarkably close with several members. I hoped one day I would be able to join their sisterhood. In spring 2019, that day came. I was initiated into the Houston Alumnae Chapter of Delta Sigma Theta Sorority, Inc.

Even though I was at PV for a brief time, I feel I have done so much. I graduated in fall 2014 with my bachelor's in marketing and

I received my Master of Business Administration in fall 2018 from my beloved alma mater. I have so many memories that I will cherish forever. I don't think I would have had this experience outside of an HBCU. I have truly learned to appreciate my culture and take pride in myself.

About Breionne Brantley

Breionne Brantley was born in Midwest City, Oklahoma on December 18th, 1990. She and her mother later moved to Kansas City, Missouri and was raised in the predominantly white suburb of Blue Springs, Missouri. Ever since she was in grade school, she fell in love with the idea of living in Texas. after countless summers spent with her grandparents. In 2009, she graduated from Blue Springs High School and moved to Garland, Texas where she attended Eastfield College. In 2010, she decided it was best to continue studies out in East Texas where she attended Texarkana College. The long nights of working a full time job and focusing on her grades granted her the chance to be accepted to attend Prairie View A&M University in fall 2012. It was then she embraced and appreciated the HBCU culture, met lifelong friends, and learned valuable lessons that would prepare her for the real world. She is a proud member of the Houston Alumnae Chapter of Delta Sigma Theta, Inc. and is currently working in the insurance field.

ANASTASIA ADAMS

The Power of Resilience

Anastasia Adams

I've always been the type of girl who was driven and hardworking, so naturally attending college was no question. Little did I know, by the time it came down to deciding where I would spend the next four years of my life, Prairie View A&M University would be my place—my home!

Freshman Year: A Girl with a Plan

Freshman year was full of self-growth. It is said that college is where you truly learn who you are and begin to develop into who you will be. Freshman year was such a scary but exciting time. I knew I had one main goal in mind. I wanted to set myself up for academic success, which meant all A's. That first semester of school, I was so focused on getting A honor roll, it seemed like all I did was go to class, the gym, the library, sleep, and repeat. But as someone who used to be a student athlete, something seemed to be missing in the equation. I quickly became homesick and had to find a way to incorporate some fun and social interaction in my focused life schedule. So, I joined the Campus Activities Board (CAB). As an introvert, being in new spaces was always nerve racking for me. It was hard putting myself out there, but CAB forced me to. CAB pretty much was the organization that organized and hosted most school-affiliated events on campus. CAB quickly became life and would continue to be in my coming years.

Sophomore Year: The Climb and the Fall

The year started off great! I was officially a Panther Advisor Leader (PAL). PALS were the campus organization tasked with the privilege of orienting incoming freshmen to campus life and culture.

We were essentially mentors and liaisons throughout their freshmen year. As a PAL, I learned so much about myself and what kind of leader I am. While juggling PALS and CAB, I also became a member of the Student Government Association (SGA). Needless to say, I was very hyperactive. With my campus involvement and extracurricular activities increasing, sophomore year was quickly showing me all the amazing opportunities and experiences that college could provide if you put yourself out there.

Just as sophomore year became an exciting year for me, it soon became one of the hardest. As a pre-nursing major, sophomore year was a fundamental foundation for the rest of my tenure at Prairie View. It was the year to complete prerequisite courses for my degree plan, take the HESI exam (the pre-nursing school entrance exam) and apply for acceptance into nursing school. In other words, it was "Go Time." Anyone who knows anything about nursing school knows that it is extremely competitive to graduate from nursing school, but it's also just as competitive to get accepted into.

During this time, my anxiety was at an all-time high, and I hadn't yet learned coping mechanisms to deal with my undiagnosed generalized anxiety. When it came time to take my HESI exam, I stressed myself out so much that I failed the anatomy and physiology portions twice, thus making me ineligible to apply for Prairie View's nursing program. This was probably one of the hardest pills for me to swallow. I was completely distraught and didn't know what to do. For the girl who currently had a 3.8 GPA, not passing your HESI was the least expected thing.

I heard of many people who had to change their major due to failing the HESI, but I never thought it would be my reality; but it was. I went to my pre-nursing advisor for guidance and her words were, "I can't tell you what to do; you have to figure it out yourself." At that moment, I realized I couldn't depend on my advisor for guidance. I couldn't depend on anyone else to get me out of this predicament. I wanted to be a registered nurse and just because PV nursing wasn't my route, didn't mean it wasn't going to happen. I was going to *find a way*. I spent the next few days trying to plan out the smartest alternative route that would lead to me achieving my RN license. I looked into several options but ultimately, I decided to stay at Prairie View and change my major.

Junior Year: The Reroute

Junior year was a transition year for me. It was the start of my first year as a health major. That year, I thought I would be in downtown Houston officially starting my nursing school journey: but it wasn't. That was okay. In my head, I had already planned out my new route; graduate from Prairie View, then apply for nursing school. That was my plan, and I was all in. I figured until it got closer for my plan to fully take its course, I was going to enjoy everything that Prairie View could offer me while maintaining my high GPA. I consumed myself in my academics, but also my organizations. I even joined Collegiate 100 and Eta Sigma Gamma National Health Honor Society. While being in these organizations, I truly got to enjoy the college experience. There was just one more thing that I wanted to achieve before my time at Prairie View ended. I wanted to be an Alpha woman.

Senior Year: I Saw the Light!

The words of my cousin continuously played in my head, "Our family only goes one way, and when you realize that, come talk to me." When she said, "only goes one way," she was referring to joining the first and finest to do it! AKA! Alpha Kappa Alpha Sorority, Inc. is the first Black intercollegiate sorority, founded on January 15, 1908. AKA was always on my mind from the time I stepped onto Prairie View's campus. I always observed the ladies on campus who were members of the sorority, and they were tough! Not only were they intelligent women who carried themselves well, but their positive impact was noticeable. After doing plenty of research on the sorority, I knew AKA was the only path for me. So, I focused my senior year on two things: AKA and graduating magna cum laude! I had to balance my time with my pursuit of being initiated into AKA, planning Springfest as an executive board member of CAB and graduation. To say I was busy would be an understatement.

With steed-fast determination, on April 2, 2017, I was initiated into the Zeta Gamma Chapter of Alpha Kappa Alpha Sorority, Inc. Oh, was that a time to be alive. With the excitement and the sense of accomplishment, it was an amazing feeling. After crossing, I quickly fell into "Greek life"—from the events to the parties and the culture. I honestly forgot I would be graduating in a short month and a half. I quickly returned to the grind and focused on the most important thing: *graduating*! After a long set of finals, I graduated from PV on May 13, 2017, magna cum laude.

After Graduation: God's Plan

After graduation, I struggled with figuring out what was next. I knew I wanted to be a nurse and the plans I had to get there, but it seemed like the route wasn't as easy as I originally planned. I went from studying for different nursing entrance exams like the TEAS, to looking for other nursing programs, and it just didn't seem right. It wasn't until my dad connected me to a nursing professor from the University of Texas at Austin, did I truly get in the right path. I took my first year after graduating from PV to focus on doing everything I needed to get accepted into UT's alternate entry MSN program. After a year of prepping and applying, I got accepted and started my journey at UT in June 2018. This would be where I would spend the next two and a half years of my life.

After a year at UT, I completed my BSN equivalent in eleven months and became a licensed registered nurse. Shortly after, I started my RN residency job full time and finished the last two years of my master's degree full-time. On December 5, 2020, I graduated cum laude from UT with my Master of Science in Nursing, with a concentration in Leadership in Diverse Settings. A year later, I began my career in travel nursing.

When I look back on my Prairie View journey, it's just a testimony of growth, trials, and tribulations; but most importantly, resilience. My experience at Prairie View gave me fun times and challenges, but it made me strong. It taught me to fight, to find a way and to make a way. Most importantly, it taught me to trust God's plan for me. No one's college journey is ever just peaches and cream. There will be trials and tribulations, but the triumph in the journey is where the success lies.

About Anastasia Adams

Anastasia Adams, MSN, RN, was born on December 25, 1994, in Austin, Texas to Carl and Althea Adams. Anastasia grew up in northeast Austin and is the youngest of four. She attended Lyndon Baines Johnson EC High School and graduated in May 2013. After graduating, Anastasia attended the illustrious Prairie View A&M University, where she received a Bachelor of Science in Health in May 2017. She would later attend the University of Texas at Austin, where she received her Master of Science in Nursing with a concentration in Leadership in Diverse Settings in December 2020. While at UT, she started her journey as a full time Registered Nurse after completing the BSN equivalent of the program in the first 11 months, then continued on to complete the rest for her MSN.

While at Prairie View, Anastasia was known as an active and involved student leader. She served as a senator in the Student Government Association, the executive secretary for the Campus Activities Board, a Panther Advisor Leader, and an active member of the Collegiate 100 and the Prairie View Student Nursing Association. In addition, Anastasia was initiated into the Zeta Gamma chapter of Alpha Kappa Alpha Sorority Inc. and Eta Sigma Gamma National Health Honor Society. While at UT, she was an active member of the Association of Nurses in Graduate School.

As a Registered Nurse, Anastasia specializes in adult acute care. While working at Ascension Seton Northwest Hospital, she received several Daisy Award nominations by patients, for providing extraordinary care. After a year and a half of bedside nursing, she started her journey as a preceptor. As a nurse preceptor she helped implement the orientation plan developed to meet each nurse's individual learning needs and helped facilitate clinical experiences. She also served as a reflective practice facilitator for Ascension Seton

RN Residency program. As a facilitator, she led reflective practice sessions that provided new residents with the opportunity to safely voice their feelings about their experiences as new RNs. In November of 2021, Anastasia took a leap of faith and began her journey as a travel nurse. As a travel nurse she lives with the mentality, "when opportunity presents itself, have the courage to go after it. Secret opportunities may be hidden inside of spaces you would never have reached if you hadn't stepped out of your comfort zone, taken a leap of faith and allowed God to lead you." Anastasia has made it her goal to help minority and underserved communities by providing patient centered, evidence-based care and encouraging people to be an active participant in their own health journey.

Aside from Anastasia's professional life, she also enjoys an active social life. Anastasia is an active member of the Beta Psi Omega chapter of Alpha Kappa Alpha Sorority Inc. and has served as the chapter's technology co-chairman. She also enjoys fellowshipping with her church family at the Church of Christ at Eastside. In addition, her hobbies include braiding hair, singing, exercising, and spending time with family and friends.

SIDNEY TAYLOR

The Road Less Traveled

Sidney Taylor

Prelude

Hey, reader! Thank you for taking the time to read my HBCU Story! I want to take you on a journey that will encourage and motivate you to never give up on your goals. No matter how hard the road is, just stick to it!

The Beginning: Why I Chose My HBCU

A native of Houston, Texas, I am actually a product of two Panthers! My parents both met at PV. Being only forty-five minutes away from Prairie View, my HBCU is highly revered in my city. Along with my parents being Panthers, many of my family members attended PV as well. Let's just say that the PV spirit ran rampant in my family.

As a child, I was always on the yard! I was the little kid running around the tailgate at homecoming. The entire HBCU experience always fascinated me. The Marching Storm, the Greeks, and the overall school spirit that the Panthers showed made an impression on me. It just looked so amazing to be a part of this big family! As I approached my senior year in high school, I began sneaking down to the yard in order to attend parties and check out the school. I knew that I found the right place to begin my college career. After graduating from Booker T. Washington High School in 2011, I promptly applied to my HBCU and was accepted!

Freshman Year: Started from the Bottom!

On August 2011, I arrived on the yard. My mother cried in my room before she left because she knew that I was taking the next step in my life. The moment she left, I had officially entered the first stage of adulthood. One of the first things that I realized was that I did not know a lot of people on the yard. I was roommates with my high school best friend, but due to his involvement with the band, I rarely saw him. If you know, you know.

For the most part, I was all alone. I knew I had to put myself out there and find good friends to hang out with. I did so by joining organizations such as The National Society of Black Engineers (NSBE) and Brothers Leading and Cultivating Knowledge (B.L.A.C.K). I surrounded myself with like-minded people, of whom I am still good friends with. I found myself having a lot of fun on the yard. I was a regular at parties, kickbacks, tailgates, and the infamous Newman Center. Once my mid-term grades came in, I learned that I needed to buckle down and hang with people who were headed towards success. Luckily, I was able to turn everything around. I attended a NSBE conference with my school and secured an internship at Hewlett Packard, where I still work to this day! I finished my freshman year with a decent GPA and an awesome internship. My journey ahead was long, but I knew that I could finish.

Sophomore/Junior Year: Big Man on Campus

I stepped back on the yard for my sophomore year with a newfound confidence. I made good money from my internship, so I was able to step up my swag a bit. Unlike the beginning of my freshman year, I had several friends who I couldn't wait to see once I got back on the yard. However, I knew that I could not play around this year. I had big aspirations. I wanted to pledge the Eta Gamma Chapter of Alpha Phi Alpha Fraternity. I knew that the chapter would have a line in the spring, so I spent the entire fall studying and picking up as many community service hours as I could. I volunteered for Meals on Wheels, Panthers at Work, and the Houston Food Bank. By the end of the fall, I had the GPA and the necessary hours to pledge. Pledging Alpha Phi Alpha was one of the best decisions I made in my life. I found myself surrounded by talented brothers who pushed me to be great. I found many opportunities to serve my community while having fun along the way. More importantly, I created a bond with my brothers that will last a lifetime.

I "stepped" back on the yard my junior year with this "Big Man on Campus" feel. I was the man! I had the internship, the frat, and the ladies in my back pocket. From shutting down step shows to throwing lit kickbacks with my frat, I definitely became engulfed in the fraternity spirit. I was the Greek that would stroll any and everywhere. In addition, I became junior class president and became step master for my frat. I must admit, I was feeling myself. As a result, I started slipping up. I found myself partying heavily and engaging in "recreational" activities, which led to me losing my Lockheed Martin internship.

Devastated, I realized that I was playing too much. I had to buckle down and get back on my purpose. I slowed down from my partying and secured a job at the library. This was by far one of the best decisions that I made in college. I was able to study all day in the quiet library. I pulled my grades back up and rededicated myself to my degree. I was able to secure my internship at Hewlett-Packard (HP) and end the year on a good note.

Senior Year(s): The Super Senior Securing the Bag!
Most engineers at PV took five to six years to graduate, and I was no exception. I didn't mind my late graduation date because I was definitely getting to the bag! Being at PV taught me how to be a hustler. I found myself co-opping during my last years at Prairie View. My internship paid me $23 an hour, which was a lot of money back in those days. In addition, I was still working in computer labs and in the outlet mall. At one point, I was working three jobs while trying to graduate. I even taught myself how to fix iPhones and started my own side hustle. To this day people still ask me to fix their phones.

I re-established myself as a leader in my fraternity and to undergraduates. I became the senator for the College of Computer Science. I found myself mentoring younger students and helping others reach their goals. I took pleasure in helping others. However, the final stretch was still not easy. I found myself taking courses at community colleges in order to get credits that I missed in school. The summer before graduation, I attended three different community colleges. I was incredibly stressed out, but I saw the light at the end of tunnel. I had an excellent job as a software engineer waiting for me at the end of the finish line, I just had to get there!

I graduated from PV in the summer of 2017 with my bachelor's degree! I remember crying in church after my college journey was all over. I had been through so much, but I made it! I couldn't help as the tears rolled down my cheeks. However, these were tears of joy! My long, rugged journey at PV made me into a man that my community would be proud of.

Aftermath

I am now gainfully employed at Hewlett Packard as an artificial intelligence sales specialist, all thanks to God my family and my HBCU! I did not want to tell a cookie cutter story about how perfect my experience was. However, I wanted to show my flaws to encourage you to keep going! This road was not easy, but I made it and you can, too.

I am a proud advocate of the HBCU experience. I encourage all to attend HBCUs and experience this amazing journey. I can depend on my memories to lift me up whenever I am feeling down. More importantly, I have made friendships that will last a lifetime. I would like to extend a big thanks to Dr. Ashley Little for allowing me to use her platform to tell my story.

About Sidney Taylor

Sidney Delante Taylor was born on October 19 1993 in Houston Texas to Yolanda McCray and Keith Taylor. He grew up in the Acres Homes neighborhood located on the North Side of the city. Although Sidney came from humble beginnings he knew that he would one day excel and become a model for his community. Sidney attended Booker T. Washington HS and graduated in 2011. He then attended Prairie View A&M University and majored in Computer Engineering. Upon graduation in August 2017, he entered the field of network administration, software engineering and cyber security. He now works at Hewlett Packard Enterprise as an Artificial Intelligence Specialist.

On campus, Sidney was known as a student leader. He served as the Junior Class President and the Senator for the College of Computer Science. During his tenure as senator, he opted for vital advancements in the Computer Science department. The bills that he proposed improved the status of the computer science department. In addition, he demonstrated great patriotism in my community by participating in several community services on and off campus. He takes pride in giving back to the community by engaging in programs such as Meals-On-Wheels and the Houston Food Bank.

Sidney has made great strides in the tech industry as well. He has worked at HPE since 2012. He has held many roles in his company such as Software Engineer, Solutions Architect, and Sales Specialist. In May 2019 he moved to the greater Atlanta area for a year in order to advance his technical skills. After this year he relocated to the Dallas area to start his career as a Sales Engineer. After seeing success in this role he was promoted to be an Artificial Intelligence Sales Specialist and finally moved back to Houston in August of

2021. Sidney has a passion for working on the cutting edge of technology and plans to eventually become a Sales Leader at a major Tech company.

Sidney also enjoys a very active social life as well. In his personal life, he enjoys boxing and MMA. He is currently a member of Katy Boxing Club. He also enjoy playing dominos and video games. He is also an active member of Alpha Phi Alpha Fraternity, Inc. He served as the Assistant Executive Director of the Texas Region, one of the highest positions available for undergraduate brothers. He also served as the step master for 3 years. He is now active in the Alpha Eta Lambda Graduate chapter here in Houston. He is also a brother of Lone Star Lodge #85 of the Most Worshipful Prince Hall Grand Lodge of Texas.

Sidney enjoys mentoring and helping others. He recently created a YouTube channel called "The ProfessionalTV". He uses his platform to help young adults succeed in their professional careers. He also mentors college students and preps their resumes. Sidney believes that helping others is a rewarding part of life and is always willing to lend a hand to someone in need.

ALAINA AARON

A New Discovery
Alaina Aaron

"Dear Prairie View, our song to thee we raise.
In gratitude, we sing our hymn of praise."

In February 2012, I stepped foot on the Prairie View A&M University campus, looking to find a home away from home. Coming from a predominantly urban high school, there was little discussion about HBCUs. An outgoing, but shy 17-year-old girl from Houston was dropped off for an anxiety provoking, but exciting experience called "Pantherland Day." During Pantherland Day, PV Cheer, the Marching Storm, and other Prairie View organizations were represented. I looked forward to orientation, Panther Camp and my first day of class. As I toured the campus as a high school senior, I knew this is where I wanted to spend the next four years. As soon as I got home that night, I applied for Prairie View with hopes of having the experience of a lifetime. In May of 2012, I received my acceptance letter, and that day changed my life forever.

Founded in 1876, Prairie View was the first state supported institution in Texas for African American students. During my time at Prairie View, I discovered the polylithic culture within the African American community. Prairie View created an environment that no matter what your history, background or beliefs are, Black people are more than their skin. Prairie View taught me black excellence. Future Black lawyers, educators, therapists, police officers, engineers, business owners, CEOs and more were being cultivated on the campus of Prairie View A & M University. Prairie View, being the second oldest public institution in Texas, held a standard of excellence in all forms. Don't get us wrong—Prairie View knows how to have a good time. Prairie View hosted a plethora of events like the *B.E.T College Tour*, Hump Day/Night, Springfest and the ultimate HBCU Homecoming—the experience that can't be explained. Experiences like these taught me the definition of being black and reinforced what that meant to me. As students, we knew how to have a good time and made sure we attended class. I would be not who I am today without the influence of Prairie View's rich history and standard of academic excellence.

During my time at Prairie View, I joined several organizations such as the Prairie View Chapter of the NAACP, Baptist Student Movement, One Accord Mime Ministry and PVAMU Concert Chorale. Additionally, I received the opportunity to travel with and represent the University. During my freshman year I traveled to North Dakota State University to represent Prairie View as a member of the Gold Members Club. I also received the opportunity to represent Prairie View as a member of the Concert Chorale and Baptist Student Movement Choir in the National Baptist Student Union Choir Competition. Prairie View also allowed me to assist in the establishment of an organization that we did not see on campus at the time. "Mentoring Incoming Freshmen" was established after my freshman year. Mentoring Incoming Freshmen focused on connecting upperclassmen and freshmen who have similar backgrounds in a mentorship. This initiative provided an opportunity for students to participate in volunteer services and leadership. As a student, I participated in convocation as a member of the Concert Chorale. We also received the opportunity to sing with composers like Jefferey Ames. Also, during my time at Prairie View I became a part of a dynamic ministry called One Accord Mime Ministry. This organization created a space for me as a student to grow in my spiritual walk and also meet women who became my sisters. One Accord mission is to ministry God's word through the art of mime. As one of the few all female religious organization on the campus of Prairie View A&M University we had an impact on not only the students but the city of Prairie View and vicinity.

Although I can't fully articulate the significance of the HBCU experience, it was definitely the experience I needed to thrive as a Black woman in America. Prairie View taught me to take pride in who I am as a Black student and future professional. From the rich history and tradition Prairie View A&M University holds to the atmosphere filled with love, joy and blackness you experience on campus is like no other. My time at Prairie View can be described with the "3 P's": Provision, Perseverance & Productivity. As a first generation HBCU graduate, Prairie View taught what perseverance means by displaying academic excellence through demanding course work. Prairie View allowed me to be a productive panther in my career, humanitarian opportunities and much more. Prairie View A&M University also allowed me to make friends that I will cherish and share fond memories for a lifetime. And because of this I have been there for weddings, graduations, birth of future Prairie View alumni and many more important life events.

Along with growing in my "blackness," I grew in leadership, academics and volunteerism as a Prairie View A &M student. Today, I am a psychotherapist working with individuals of various backgrounds, religions, and races; however, my primary focus is helping people of color who are homeless or reside in low economic areas. Currently we are working with the state to fund family who have been affected tremendously by the Covid-19 pandemic. I am also the creator of "Mental Wellness 4 Millennials," a platform focused on providing mental health & wellness resources for millennials who deal with mental and emotional struggles. You may ask, "What does my future look like?" In the future Mental Wellness 4 Millennials will provide workshops and seminars in low-income community that focus on mental wellness practices and resource education. I would also like to give back and teach in higher level education at an HBCU. I am also an active volunteer for the Star of Hope Women's Shelter. As an active member of my local PVAMU Alumni Chapter, I can give back to my university through giving and mentoring current students and now share my experiences with you all. Prairie View is and will always be the place to be.

"We'll love thee now, and through eternity."
Alaina Aaron, M.A. LPC Associate
Class of 2016; B. S. in Criminal Justice & Juvenile Justice

About Alaina Aaron

Alaina Aaron, M.A. is a native Houstonian who started her journey at Prairie View A&M University in Fall 2016 as an incoming freshman. Alaina quickly became a part of the PVAMU family participating in the UC Freshmen Step Team, Baptist Student Union and PVAMU Concert Chorale. By her sophomore year Alaina and a close friend (Benicia C) decided to create an organization that helped mentor freshmen on a one-on-one level. Mentoring Incoming Freshmen, a.k.a M.I.F., began in Fall 2013 and continues to be a major part of the freshmen experience today. Alaina also participated in Tor De Pink, Panthers at Work, SGA "Rock the Vote" Committee. March of Dimes and Relay 4 Life. Alaina was a member of One Accord Mime Ministry, Criminal Justice Club, Prairie View Young Democrats and PVAMU Chapter of the NAACP. Alaina's time at Prairie View made her who she is today. Alaina received her Bachelor of Science degree in Criminal Justice-Juvenile Justice in Spring of 2016 and a Master of Arts degree in Clinical Mental Health Counseling in Fall of 2020 from Houston Baptist University. Today, Alaina is a provisionally license therapist in the state of Texas. Alaina is also the creator of Mental Wellness 4 Millennials, which focuses on providing mental health & wellness psychoeducation for those who face every day mental & emotional struggles. Alaina is an advocate of Mental Health & Wellness education specifically among the African American community. During her free time, she volunteers at the Star of Hope Women's shelter and enjoying time spent with friends & family.

DR. COREY SHY

Breeding Success
Dr. Corey Shy

"I became a doctor by accident"

At least that's what I told myself. Growing up in a small town like St. Martin, Mississippi, I never dreamed about being a doctor. Honestly, I don't know anyone who wanted to become a doctor or thought that they could become one. At age fifteen, I moved to Lufkin, Texas—another small town, after Hurricane Katrina. Again, I was exposed to medicine; however, becoming a doctor really wasn't a thing. In school, I was pretty smart but didn't apply myself and teachers knew that. So, all of my evaluations would mention, "he has potential."

When I took biology in the tenth grade, that's when I recognized my potential. I loved the topics, and the material came easy to me. It was also probably because this was the first Black teacher I ever had in my life. She knew that I was smart and told me one day that I really should be in her Pre AP class.

"Naw, I'm good. Those kids are lame, and all my friends and teammates are in regular classes," I responded to her. So, she went to my parents and told them. They gave me the ultimatum of either quitting football or taking Pre-AP chemistry the next year. I was about to start varsity, so there was no way I was quitting football. The following year, to my surprise, I did well in the class, earning a B+. That's when my mentality shifted. I realized that it's okay to be smart and you can still be cool.

Inspired by my biology teacher, I decided that I wanted to be a high school biology teacher. I thought I could be a biology teacher with an education major and biology minor; however, while doing my degree plan, I was told that I had to major in biology. Then, they showed me the degree plan. My dad and I saw all of those intense science classes. As a joke, he said, "Boy, you might as well be a doctor."

I always desired to attend an HBCU. Both of my parents went to Southern University, and my grandfather went to Tougaloo College. Attending *Battle of the Bands* was one of my most anticipated events when I lived on the Gulf Coast. My father took my sister and I along with busloads of kids from our high school to HBCU colleges to get the much-needed exposure. At my high school, the counselors did not encourage us to go to HBCUs. They treated them as "good back-up plans" if you couldn't get into some of the PWI colleges and maybe above our community college. After going on a few school tours, I knew Prairie A&M University was the school for me. What stood out to me was its beautiful campus, the school pride and spirit, and the reputation of its alumni. I'd be fooling myself if I didn't mention the pretty women. I remember some of my friends teased me about choosing an HBCU, saying things like, "It's only a party school" and "My degree would be worthless." You can only imagine what those same people are doing today.

When I got to Prairie View A&M University, I was in a huge auditorium for Biology 1, and everyone else was some pre-health major. I was the only one who wanted to be a teacher. I joined the pre-med organization—not because I wanted to be a doctor (I was actually scared of blood at that point). It was because all my friends were in it, and I didn't want to feel left out.

I was exposed to the field of medicine and had great upperclassmen mentors who gave me the confidence and resources that encouraged me to become a doctor. Nevertheless, I still didn't want to be a medical doctor. I was thinking maybe PT or chiropractor because again, I was scared of blood. They told me to apply to this summer program called Summer Medical Dental and Enrichment Program (SMDEP). They said it was guaranteed to change my life. I did the program at Yale and that's when I knew that medicine was for me.

More importantly, it gave me the confidence that I would be able to achieve that goal.

However, everything wasn't peaches and cream after that. After studying intensely for my MCAT for two straight years, taking multiple review courses, and over twenty practice tests I did not do well on my MCAT. I didn't think I was going to get into medical school, but at that point, I had nothing to lose. To my surprise, I was accepted into Texas A&M Health Science Center. I received the award for best performing student while attending a summer program after my sophomore year. They decided to give me a chance despite my MCAT scores.

Going from a Prairie View to Texas A&M was a big demographic shift, but Prairie View prepared me to be successful in any environment. I was the only Black male in my medical school class of 200 students. Also, I was the only Black male in my residency class of fifty people.

It has always been my passion to give back and try to get more underrepresented minorities into medicine, particularly Black males. I worked on multiple initiatives and programs with one in particular that is dear to me called Tour4Diversity in Medicine. This was an organization co-founded by a HBCU and Prairie alumni, Dr. Alden Landry. Nationally recognized, Tour4Diversity in Medicine's mission is to help recruit more URM to help change the face of medicine.

I am still close to the friends and Alpha Phi Alpha Fraternity brothers I met while I was at PV. We are all successful in different fields including physicians, dentistry, pharmacy, engineering, teachers, business professionals and entrepreneurs. We have weekly book clubs and Zoom sessions, and we go on at least one to two trips a year. I honestly think I would have not had the quality of education, experience, and friendships if I did not go to an HBCU. When I have kids, I hope the HBCU tradition can continue.

I'll close with the saying we like to say at PV but can be applied to HBCUs as a whole: *Prairie View Produces Productive People.*

About Dr. Corey Shy

Dr. Corey Shy was born in Decatur, Georgia in 1991 and moved to Biloxi, Mississippi in 1995 where he stayed until 2005 before moving to Lufkin, Texas where he graduated from Lufkin High school in 2009. He went on to pursue a bachelor of science in Biology with a minor in chemistry at Prairie View A&M University where he graduated Magna Cum Laude in May 2013. There he was very involved in on campus activities including being a member of Alpha Phi Alpha fraternity, President of Minority of Association of Premedical Students while during his tenure won organization of the year, and the Undergraduate Medical Academy to name a few.

In 2013 he enrolled in medical school at Texas A&M Health Science Center (TAMHSC). There he was the only black male in his class of 200 people. He was elected as class CEO of his medical school class for both the 2013 and 2014 academic year and also reenacted the Student National Medical Association (SNMA) on the medical campus and started the Minority Association of Medical Students (MAPS) on the Texas A&M undergrad campus. In 2014 he also served as the Regional MAPS liaison, won regional member of the year for SNMA, and was a presenter at the national meeting. In 2016 he was inducted into Gold Humanism Honor Society. In May 2017 he graduated from TAMHSC.

He went on to complete his internship and residency in Internal Medicine at Washington University School of Medicine in St. Louis / Barnes-Jewish Hospital from 2017-2020. During his time at Washington University he served as the resident leader for the Gateway 180 woman and children homeless shelter where he hosted health talks to the residents and helped coordinate health fairs. He was also the co-president of Washington University Minority Medical Association (WUMMA). This is an organization for residents and fellows at Wash U that assist in the recruitment of underrepresented minority residents and fellows and help the professional development of its members. During residency Dr. Shy was exposed to multiple specialties and research opportunities but ultimately discovered a passion for treating and managing a broad spectrum of diseases in an inpatient setting.

He joined the faculty as an instructor in the Department of Medicine in the Division of Hospital Medicine at Washington University School of Medicine/Barnes-Jewish Hospital in June 2020. He has served on multiple committees since starting including Diversity, equity inclusion committee (DEI), Recruitment committee, and is involved with medical student and residency training. He is also a longstanding mentor for Tour 4 Diversity. This organization does bus tours (currently virtual) to different HBCUs and colleges with high URM populations hosting conferences and workshops to help increase the amount of URM in the health care field. In his spare time Dr. Shy enjoys golfing, book club, traveling, collecting sneakers, and personal finances and investing. You can follow him on IG @phisician.

Official Partners & Sponsors
of The HBCU Experience Movement, LLC

According to RP Podcast
CEO/Founder: Ritha Pierre, Esq.
@accordingtorp
accordingtorp@gmail.com

ACTIVate
CEO/Founder: Yladera Drummond, J.D.
contact@activateleadership.org
info@yladeradrummond.com
www.yladeradrummond.com
www.activateleadership.org

AC Events
The Luxury Planning Experience
CEO/Founder: Amy Agbottah
amy@amycynthiaevents.com

Alexander G. Events
CEO/Founder: Nathan Alexander Kemp
Nathan A. Kemp, 336-706-1422
Brooke G. Kemp, 336-944-4768
alexgevents20@gmail.com

AMMEA
President: Ernest Stackhouse
ej.stackhouse@gmail.com
www.ammea.org

Allen Financial Solutions
CEO/Founder: Jay Allen
@jay83allen
@Jay Allen
allen.jonathan83@gmail.com

The Ancestor Key
CEO/Founder: Ja'el Gordon
504-356-1466
theancestor@gmail.com

The Alli Group, LLC
Real Estate Management
Founders: Lawrence & Nickia Alli
@thealligroupllc
nickia.alli@gmail.com
www.thealligroupllc.com

Ashley Little Enterprises, LLC
CEO/Founder: Dr. Ashley Little
@_ashleyalittle
@Ashley Little
aalittle08@gmail.com
www.ashleylittleenterprises.com

The Self-care Doc

CEO/Founder:

Dr. Raushannah Johnson-Verwayne
*Licensed Clinical Psychologist &
Wellness Coach*

 @Ask Dr RJ

@Ask Dr RJ

www.AskDrRJ.com

The Black Techies/Podcast

CEO/Founder: Herbert L. Seward, III
*Where black culture meets the world
of technology.*

www.theblacktechies.com

Assurance Tax & Accounting Group, LLC

CEO/Founder:

Kimberlee Collins-Walker

8676 Goodwood Blvd., Ste. 102

Baton Rouge, LA 70876

225-757-7518

kim@assurancetaxbr.com

www.assurancetaxbr.com

BLKWOMENHUSTLE

CEO/Founder: Lashawn Dreher

@blkwomenhustle

@Blk Women Hustle

info@blkwomenhustle.com

Baker & Baker Realty, LLC

CEO/Founder: Christopher Baker

@seedougieblake

@Christopher D. Baker

baker.christopher@gmail.com

Block Band Music & Publishing, LLC

CEO/Founder: D. Rashad Watters

919-698-2560

blockbandmusic@gmail.com

Boardroom Brand, LLC

CEO/Founder: Samuel Brown, III

📷 @_gxxdy

✉️ samuel.brown.three@gmail.com

booked cafe
children's diverse bookshop

Booked Cafe Books

CEO/Founder: Kierra Jones

📷 @Booked Cafe Books

📘 @Booked Cafe Books

✉️ contact@bookedcafebooks.com

🌐 www.bookedcafebooks.com

Bound By Conscious Concepts

CEO/Founder: Kathryn Lomax

📷 @msklovibes223

📘 @Klo-Kathryn Lomax

📠 972-638-9823

✉️ klomax@bbconcepts.com

Brooks Art Collective

CEO/Founder: LaToya Brooks

📷 @brooksartcollective

📘 @brooksartcollective

✉️ brooksartcollective@gmail.com

CAFÉ SAINT-EX
RESTAURANT | BAR

Campaign
Engineers

Campaign Engineers

CEO/Founder: Chris Smith

📷 @csmithatl

✉️ csmithl911@gmail.com

Chef Batts
CEO/Founder: Keith Batts
@ @chefbatts
✉ booking@chefbatts.com

Color Wheel Therapy
CEO/Founder: Kiandra Daniels
☎ 469-251-2418
✉ kiandra.daniels@colorwheeltherapy.com
🌐 www.colorwheeltherapy.com

Cici's Freelance Services
CEO/Founder:
  Courtney "Cici" Walker, MPA
@ @cicisfreelanceservices
☎ 225-288-8216
✉ cicisfreelanceservices@gmail.com

Commit 2 Life Fitness
CEO/Founder: Joseph T. Shaw III
@ @commit2lifefitness
The Bitter Suite Podcast
Apple & Spotify
@ @thebittersuite2020
🌐 www.commit2life.com

Cjenk The Agency: Creative Concierge, LLC
CEO/Founder: Chasmin Jenkins
✉ chasminjenkins@gmail.com

Curves & Gangs
CEO/Founder: Patrice Murphy
@ @curvesandgaines
✉ curvesandgains@gmail.com
🌐 www.curvesandgains.com

DD Jones Enterprise

CEO/Founder: Darcele Jones-Horton

✉ darceleh@bellsouth.net

Enlightened Visions, Inc.

CEO/Founder: TaNisha Fordham

✉ tanisha.fordham@gmail.com

🌐 www.enlightenedvisions.org

Deroune Services, LLC

CEO/Founder: Marina Zeno

📱 337-418-0785

Executive Reign

CEO/Founder: Canisha Cierra Turner

📘 @Executive Reign

📱 804-605-6875

🌐 www.executivereign.com

🌐 www.canishacierraturner.com

Eclectikread Marketing

CEO/Founder: Christa Newkirk

📷 @chris_ta_da

✉ info@eclectikread.com

February First

CEO/Founder: Cedric Livingston

Director/Writer: *February First: A Stride Towards Freedom*

🌐 www.februaryfirstmovie.com

engHERneered

CEO/Founder: Christina Caldwell, PE

✉ engherneered@gmail.com

Freeda's World Podcast
CEO/Founder: Ritha Pierre, Esq.
📷 @freedas_world
✉️ accordingtorp@gmail.com

Give Black App
Co-Founder/COO: Alexus Hall
📷 @giveblackapp
📘 @Give Black App
🐦 @giveblackapp
🌐 www.giveblackapp.com

HBCU 101
CEO/Founder: Jahliel Thurman
📷 @HBCU101
✉️ jahlielthurman@gmail.com
🌐 www.hbcu101.com

Happy Hour Investors
Co-Founder/Managing Partner:
Jonathan Rivers
830 Glenwood Ave., Ste. 510-352
Atlanta, GA 30316
☎️ 404-860-2288
✉️ jonathan@hhinvestors.com
🌐 www.hhinvestors.com

Harbor Institute
CEO/Founder:
Rasheed Ali Cromwell, J.D.
📷 @theharborinstitute
📘 @The Harbor Institute
🐦 @harborinstitute
✉️ racromwell@theharborinstitute.com

THE HBCU
BAND
EXPERIENCE
WITH CHRISTY WALKER

The HBCU Band Experience with Christy Walker
CEO/Founder: Dr. Christy Walker
✉️ christywalker57@gmail.com
🌐 www.christywalker.com

HBCU Buzz
(HBCU Buzz | Taper, Inc. | Root Care Health)
CEO/Founder: Luke Lawal, Jr.
📷 @lukelawal
📘 @L & COMPANY
📠 301-221-1719
✉️ lawal@lcompany.co

HBCU Girls Talk
CEO/Founder: TeeCee Camper
📷 @HBCUgirlstalk
✉️ talkgirls@yahoo.com

HBCU Cheer Black Excellence
📷 @HBCUcheer
✉️ HBCUcheerleaders@yahoo.com

HBCU Grad
CEO/Founder: Todd Finley
📠 312-535-8511
🌐 www.hbcugraduates.com

The HBCU Experience Movement, LLC
CEO/Founder: Dr. Ashley Little
📷 @_ashleyalittle
📘 @DrAshley Little
✉️ thehbcuexperiencemovement@gmail.com
🌐 www.thehbcuexperiencemovement.com

HBCU Legacy Fashion
CEO/Founder: Cheylaina Fultz
📷 @HBCULegacyFashion
📘 @HBCULegacyFashion
✉️ contact@hbculegacyfashion.com
🌐 www.hbculegacyfashion.com

HBCU Pride Nation
CEO/Founder: Travis Jackson
📷 @HBCUpridenation
📘 @HBCU Pride Nation
✉ travispjackson@gmail.com

HBCU Wall Street
CEO/Founders:
  Torrence Reed & Jamerus Peyton
📘 @HBCU Wall Street
✉ info@hbcuwallstreet.com

HBCU Pulse
CEO/Founder: Randall Barnes
📷 @HBCUpulse
🐦 @thehbcupulse
🌐 www.hbcupulse.com

H.E.R. Story Podcast
H.E.R. Story with J. Jamison
CEO/Founder: Janea Jamison
📷 @herstory _podcast
#Herstorymovement

HBCU Times
CEO/Founders: David Staten, Ph. &
Bridget Hollis Staten, Ph.D
📷 @HBCU_times8892
📘 @HBCU Times
✉ hbcutimes@gmail.com

Holistic Practitioners
CEO/Founder: Tianna Bynum
📘 @Tianna Bynum
✉ tpb33@georgetown.edu

ICG Marriage & Family Therapy
CEO/Founders:
  Jabari & Stephanie Walthour
📷 @thedopesextherapist
✉ stephanie@intimacycenterga.com
🌐 www.intimacycenterga.com

J.Robins CPA, LLC
CEO/Founder: Joseph Robins
📷 @robinscpa
📘 @jrobinscpa
9800 Line Hwy., Ste. 261
Baton Rouge, LA 70816
📠 225-650-7306
✉ info@jrobinscpa.com
🌐 www.jrobinscpa.com

Johnson Capital
CEO/Founder: Marcus Johnson
📷 @marcusdiontej
✉ marcus@johnsoncap.com

Kelly Collaborative Medicine
CEO/Founder: Dr. Kathyrn Kelly
10801 Lockwood Dr., Ste. 160
Silver Spring, MD 20901
📠 301-298-1040
🌐 www.kellymedicinemd.com

Journee Enterprises
CEO/Founder: Fred Whit
📷 @frederickwjr
📘 @Fred Whit
✉ frederickwjr@yahoo.com

K.Y. Turner Law Firm, PLLC
CEO/Founder: Khanay Turner, Esq.
✉ khanay.turner@icloud.com

The Lady BUGS

CEO/Founder: Tatiana Tinsley Dorsey

@theladybugsoffical

@HBCU Times

ladybugs_HQ@googlegroups.com

Swing Into Their Dreams Foundation

Co-Founders: Pamela Parker and
Lynn Demmons

swingintotheirdreams@gmail.com

www.swingintotheirdreams.com

LEMM Media Group

CEO/Founder: Cremel Nakia Burney

@cremel_the_creator

cremelburney@gmail.com

LK Productions

CEO/Founder: Larry King

@lk_rrproduction

@Larry King

lkproduction@yahoo.com

Little Publishing, LLC

CEO/Founder: Dr. Ashley Little

@_ashleyalittle

@DrAshley Little

info@ashleyalittle.com

www.ashleylittleenterprises.com

Lynch Law, PLLC

CEO/Founder: Chance D. Lynch, Esq.

1015A Roanoke Ave., Ste. A

Roanoke Rapids, NC 27870

252-535-1251

The Marching Force
700 Emancipation Dr.
Hampton, VA 23668
🌐 www.supportthematchingforce.com

The Marching Podcast
CEO/Founder: Joseph Beard
✉ marchingpodcast@gmail.com
🌐 www.themarchingpodcast.com

Marching Sport
CEO/Founder: Gerard Howard
✉ gerardhoward@gmail.com

McKallen Medical
CEO/Founder: Sade Stephenson,
    MSN, RN, AGACNP-BC
9253 Hermosa Ave., Ste. B
Rancho Cucamonga, CA 91730
☎ 747-225-6776
✉ mckallenmedical@gmail.com
🌐 www.mckallenmedicaltraining.com

**Minority Cannabis Business
Association**
President: Shanita Penny
📷 @Minority Cannabis
📘 @MCBA.Org
🐦 @MinCannBusAssoc
💼 @Minority Cannabis Business
    Association
☎ 202-681-2889
✉ info@minoritycannabis.org
🌐 www.minoritycannabis.org

Mills Academy
CEO/Founder: Airneica Mills
📇 662-822-6976
✉ millsacademy1@gmail.com

Never2Fly2Pray
CEO/Founder: Jeffrey Lee Sawyer
📷 @never2fly2pray
📘 @Jeffrey Lee
✉ htdogwtr@yahoo.com

MilRo Entertainment
CEO/Founder: Chevis Anderson
✉ milrosplace@yahoo.com

NXLevel Travel (NXLTRVL)
CEO: Hercules Conway
📷 @herc3k
📘 @Hercules Conway
COO: Newton Dennis
📷 @nxlevel
📘 @Newton Dennis
✉ info@nxleveltravel.com
🌐 www.nxleveltravel.com

NC Dance District
CEO/Founder: Dr. Kellye Worth Hall
📷 @divadoc5
📘 @Kellye Worth Hall
✉ delta906@gmail.com

OEDM Group
CEO/Principal Owner: Justin Blake
📷 @oedmgroup.com
✉ contact@oedmgroup.com
🌐 www.oedmgroup.com

PacketStealer Gaming
CEO/Founder: David Matthews
✉ packetstealer@outlook.com

━ WASHINGTON DC ━

PILAR
Co-Owner: Nate Perry
📷 @barpilar
✉ nate@pilardc.com

The Perfect Glow
CEO/Founder: Berrie Russell
✉ berrierussell@gmail.com
🌐 www.tpglow.com

Queen Series
CEO/Founder: Randall Barnes
✉ aqueenseries@gmail.com

The Phoenix Professional Network
CEO/Founder: DJavon Alston
📷 @thephoenixnetwork757
f @DJavon Alston
✉ thephoenixnetwork757@gmail.com

Raggedi Luxury Durags
CEO/Founder: Chasmin Jenkins
✉ chasminjenkins@gmail.com

Reid Creative Solutions, LLC
CEO/Founder: Aja Reid
📠 919-822-2892
✉ info@reidcreativesolutions.com
🌐 www.reidcreativesolutions.com

Shani L., Relationship Enthusiast
CEO/Founder: Shani L.Farmer
📷 @shanilrelationshipenthusiast
✉ info@shanilfarmer.com
🌐 www.shanilfarmer.com

SayYes

Say Yes, LLC
CEO/Founder: Porscha Lee Taylor
📷 @sayyesplanners
✉ info@sayyescareer.com
🌐 www.sayyesplanners.com

She Is Magazine
CEO/Founder: Ciara Horton
📷 @sheisemagazine
📘 @Ciara Horton
✉ ciarasheisemagazine.com

SC DJ WORM 803
CEO/Founder: Jamie Brunson
📷 @SCDJWORM803
📘 @SC DJ Worm 803
🐦 @SCDJWORM803
Ⓜ @SC DJ Worm 803
✉ scdjworm803@gmail.com
🌐 www.scdjworm803.com

Southern University A&M College
801 Harding Blvd.
Baton Rouge, LA 70807
📠 225-771-4500

Southern University Alumni Federation
124 Roosevelt Steptoe Dr.
Baton Rouge, LA 70807
📠 225-771-4200
✉ sualumni@sualumni.org

Springbreak Watches (SPGBK)
CEO/Founder: Kwame Molden
📷 @SPGBK
📘 @Kwame Molden
✉ info@springbreakwatches.com

Success and Religion
CEO/Founder: Micheal Taylor
✉ successismyreligion@gmail.com

Sugar Top Spirit & Beverage Co.
CEO/Founder: Terri White
📷 @sugartopspirits
🐦 @sugartopspirits
✉ tl.white412@gmail.com
🌐 www.sugartopspirits.com

Stamp'd Travel
CEO/Founder:
   Jocelyn Hadrick Alexander
📷 @jocehadyou
✉ jocelyn.h.alexander@gmail.com
🌐 www.stampdtravel.com

SwagHer
Vice President of Sales / Marketing:
   Jarmel Roberson
📷 @swaghermagazine
✉ jroberson@swagher.net
🌐 www.swagher.net

TLW Photography
CEO/Founder: Taylor Whitehead
✉ mrknowitall91@aol.com

Uplift Clothing Apparel
CEO/Founder: Jermaine Simpson
📷 @upliftclothingapparel
🌐 www.upliftclothingapparel.com

Upward Path
CEO/Founder:
   Cameron Chalmers Dupree
📷 @upwardpathtc
✉ contact@upwardpathtc.com
🌐 www.upwardpathtc.com

The Urban Learning &
Leadership Center, Inc.

The Urban Learning &
   Leadership Center, Inc.
President/Co-Founder:
   John W. Hodge, Ed.D
✉ jhodge@ulleschools.com

The Vernon Group
   Cooperative Solutions
CEO/Founder: Anthony V. Stevens
📷 @investednu
✉ info@vernongroupllc.com

Vision Tree, LLC
CEO/Founder: Dr. Jorim Reed
📷 @upwardpathtc
✉ visiontreellc@gmail.com

VJR Real Estate
CEO/Founder: Victor Collins, Jr.
📷 @vjrtherealtor
✉️ vic@thevjrgroup.com

Yard Talk 101
CEO/Founder: Jahliel Thurman
📷 @YardTalk101
🌐 www.yardtalk101.com

We Are Educated, Inc.

We Are Educated, Inc.
CEO/Founder: Ayanna Spivey
📷 @ayannaceleste
✉️ ayanna.spivey@yahoo.com

Zoom Technologies, LLC
CEO/Founder: Torrence Reed
📷 @torrencereed3
✉️ support@zoom-technologies.co

Yard Stubs
CEO/Founder: Cremel Burney
📷 @YardStubs
✉️ partnerships@yardstubs.com
🌐 www.yardstubs.com

Made in the USA
Coppell, TX
28 April 2022

77154723R00160